MINDFUL MASTERY

Find Focus, Get Unstuck, and Drop Into the Peak Performance Zone

WIL DIECK

Cover Design: Pagatana Design—pagatana.com
Book Interior and E-book Design by Amit Dey—amitdey2528@gmail.com
Publishing Consultant: Geoff Affleck—geoffaffleck.com

TMT Publications

ISBN: 978-0-9963072-5-3 (p)
ISBN: 978-0-9963072-6-0 (e)

Get Your Mindful Mastery Journal!

To get the most of this book you're going to need a journal.

One of the best things you can do to improve yourself is to record the feedback you get from your efforts, think about it, and then decide how you are going to use that feedback in the future. This is why you should have a journal.

I highly suggest you use a journal to record the feedback you get while going through the exercises in this book so you can track your progress. To help you, I've created an interactive journal you can use just for this purpose.

Go to https://tinyurl.com/Mindful-Mastery-Journal to get your FREE interactive journal especially designed for this book!

About the Author

*A*uthor, speaker, college professor and researcher, Wil Dieck is also a master hypnotherapist, NLP Trainer and master martial arts instructor. His educational background and extensive martial arts training coalesce to give his students and readers a rich framework from which to learn. He is currently a professor of psychology and business at San Diego University for Integrated Studies.

For the past 40 years, Wil has taught people, from a variety of backgrounds, how to use simple mind hacking techniques to create habits of success.

Sharing his expertise, Wil runs a leadership and peak performance coaching practice in San Diego, California. He helps his clients create the belief systems of successful people and leaders, allowing them to make the most of their personal and professional lives.

He is the founder of the educational organization Black Belt Breakthroughs, and has taught hundreds of people in individual and business settings how to use Mindful Mind Hacking techniques to strengthen their mind's abilities to focus on getting the most they can out of life.

Wil is available for individual coaching sessions and group presentations. He shares how to use Mindful Mind Hacking to develop the habits of success. Connect with Wil at mindfulmindhacking.com.

Contents

Acknowledgments

While there are many people who through some manner or another have contributed to this book, I want to acknowledge the few who were instrumental to its completion.

First, to my partner in crime, Lynette Seid, who encourages me in so many ways every day. I love you. Thank you from the bottom of my heart for your love and support.

Second to my two children, Vanessa and Samuel Dieck, who have inspired me in so many ways. Thank you for being you.

Finally, I dedicate this to you, the reader. As I wrote this book, I always tried to keep you in mind. Thank you for trusting me and reading this book. This means the world to me.

Why Should You Read This Book?

"You have considerable power to construct self-helping thoughts, feelings and actions as well as to construct self-defeating behaviors. You have the ability, if you use it, to choose healthy instead of unhealthy thinking, feeling and acting."

- Albert Ellis

How's your life been lately? Is it running along smoothly or is it busy and complicated?

In today's world, if you're like most people, you probably feel like your life is spinning around like a hamster wheel.

Because of life's speed today, you're probably being adversely affected by all types of emotions. Emotions like anxiety, fear, dread, anger, rage, frustration, disappointment and even sorrow and grief.

After a while, these negative, disempowering emotions can begin to weigh you down, affecting you for hours, days, weeks or even months on end. The never-ending onslaught on your senses makes you feel overwhelmed, exhausted, frustrated. It even makes some people depressed. Others are driven to want it all to end.

What if you could learn a set of skills that could turn all of this around? Skills that can help you control your thinking and emotions?

Would those skills be worth learning?

You're probably saying, "Well, heck yeah!"

You might also be thinking, "Are there really skills like that?

The answer is a resounding "YES!"

In this book you're going to discover the greatest tool on earth. You're also going to learn skills you can use that will give you the ability to master the operation of this tool. These skills will help you control your thinking and emotions and live a happier, healthier, more success-filled life.

This might sound unbelievable, but the ability to control your thinking and emotions helps you take control of how you respond to all the different and unpleasant situations that regularly pop up in your life. The way you respond to these situations is not only the secret to happiness, but also the secret to being able to get whatever you want out of life.

Why?

It's because the quality of your life depends on your perspective. The lens you see the world through is how you interpret the events in your life.

It's your interpretation of these events, more than the events themselves, that control how you feel. Your interpretation creates your mood and your mood affects your performance.

Why's that?

Because different emotions create different neurotransmitters, or drugs your brain manufactures on an almost a moment-to-moment basis. The problem is that negative emotions can manufacture drugs that stress you out, narrow your focus and wipe out your perceptive.

Here's how these drugs work.

Let's say you're enjoying a pleasant drive on a beautiful road that overlooks the ocean. Suddenly, "wham!" a car sideswipes you, flips your car over and sends your car through the guardrail.

Now you're upside-down, hanging over a ledge. You realize that any slight movement could upset your balance and send you plunging down the cliff to your death (I didn't say this was going to be a pleasant scenario).

What happens to you?

You freeze because you don't want to tumble down the cliff. Simultaneously, your brain sends signals to your body to activate one of its superpowers, the fight, freeze or flight system.

Your fight, freeze or flight system causes certain neurons in your brain to fire, releasing neurotransmitters. These neurotransmitters are drugs like dopamine, cortisol and norepinephrine. Drugs that get you ready to fight or flee.

Meanwhile, your sympathetic nervous system also responds. It begins producing chemicals of its own. Specifically, a part of your brain, called the adrenal medulla, will secrete adrenaline and noradrenaline.

The release of these chemicals—the body's natural drugs—will cause numerous physiological changes in your body. Your heartrate increases, your muscles contract and your mind races. Left unchecked, these drugs can send your brain spinning out of control, just like the car in the scenario.

But it turns out this is your lucky day. The fire and rescue station is located just around the next bend and they heard the sound of the accident. They respond immediately to the accident scene. Within seconds of the accident, and, without your knowledge (you had hit your head after all), they attached a tow chain to your car.

You're not in danger, you're completely safe.

The truth is, since you didn't know they'd attached the chain, your brain and body went into overdrive. You believed you could die. Your body's reaction was in response to your perception. Not to your reality.

What does this have to do with you and your life?

When you begin to examine your life, what you'll find is there are many scenarios where you believe you're in more danger than you really are.

Just like if you were upside down hanging over a cliff in your car, it's your belief of the danger you're in that launches your body's fight, freeze or flight superpower. While this is a good superpower if you are really in danger, it can be unquestionably dangerous to your psychological and physical health if you're not.

What would happen if you could learn to control your thinking and take charge of your emotional responses? How would your life be different?

For one, you could prevent repeatedly automatically activating your fight, freeze or flight system. Instead of turning into a raging lunatic (as some people do), you could stay calm and focused.

You'll also receive other benefits from your ability to control your emotions, such as enhancing your self-confidence.

With increased confidence, you'll start seeing more opportunities. Your new perspective makes you more productive and more successful. It can even help you to become wealthier.

And it doesn't stop there.

Controlling your thinking and emotions means you'll be less anxious. You'll be able to overcome your fears and phobias.

It allows you to live a more harmonious life. This is because being in charge of your emotions can help you avoid arguments that can turn into shouting matches with your spouse, children and co-workers. How does this sound to you?

What about having more energy—wouldn't that be a good thing? Controlling your thinking will free up energy you used to waste on unproductive thoughts. Now you'll feel more powerful and be more efficient.

Not only that, you'll be able to drop into certain moods on demand. Moods you can use to tap into crystal clear thinking and superhuman strength.

In this book you're going to learn how to get the most out of your life by learning how to drop into the zone, anytime and anyplace. This allows you to maximize the power of the greatest tool on earth, a tool you've had available to you since birth.

This tool is your brain.

You're going to do this by learning skills that will help you control your focus, thinking, and as a result, your emotions. Using what you're going to learn in this book you'll be able to drop into the zone the same way black belts, top athletes and all peak performers do.

Why is being able to drop into the zone so important?

It's because, in the zone, you can maximize your focus, supercharge your success and add more peace and calm to your life.

Does this sound like it's too good to be true?

I guarantee it's not.

Because by learning to control your thinking you can, like all highly successful people, drop into the zone, anytime and anyplace you need to, and on demand.

Good things happen in the zone.

Instead of being frozen by problems, you're able to quickly analyze and move through them. These are the same problems that used to keep you from accomplishing the great things in life you want to achieve.

That's what Mindful Mind Mastery is all about. Learning how to drop into the zone and function in a peak performance state.

This state is the secret to being able to do whatever it takes to get things done.

Mindful Mind Mastery is about giving you the skills you need to enter this state. The state that allows you to accomplish the great things you want to achieve.

This Isn't Complicated

As a nearly life-long martial artist, I wrote this book like a good martial arts system. Each lesson is designed to build upon the previous ones so you can develop and hone your skills.

The information you'll find here is as simple as it is possible but still contains all the elements you need to become a highly skilled.

This book follows the principle: to "make," as Einstein said, "things as simple as possible, but no simpler."

Are you ready to get started?

All right then, let's begin!

Chapter 1

Flow State – AKA "The Zone"

"Control of consciousness determines the quality of life."

— **Dr. Mihaly Csikszentmihalyi**

When you hear the term "flow," it sounds a bit strange, right? Maybe it conjures up images of something Zen-like, where your mind is empty, and you're only focused on one thing—your breathing.

A meditation of sorts.

While being in the flow can feel like meditation, meditating doesn't necessarily put you in the zone.

Here's a brief explanation of what it's like to be in the flow state:

"When you're in flow state, you're completely engaged in the task at hand, to the point where you lose track of time. You experience great joy simply in doing the job before you. Everything else fades into the background as you focus on what needs to be done immediately, in this moment. This focus is so intense that you block out all distractions while working on that one all important task."

Entering the flow state is a completely immersive experience. In the zone, you are fully committed to what you're doing in this moment in time.

There is no room in your consciousness for anything else besides what you are doing right now. Everything else in your environment fades to the background. This is the flow state, AKA the zone. It is the land where the highest performers dwell.

This is the place where you have the motivation and energy to accomplish nearly anything you choose. The place of total immersion.

Total Immersion

Dr. Mihaly Csikszentmihalyi is credited for discovering the psychological concept of flow. In his book Flow: The Psychology of Optimal Experience, Dr. Csikszentmihalyi writes:

"I developed a theory of optimal experience based on the concept of flow - the state in which people are so involved in an activity that nothing else seems to matter; the experience itself is so enjoyable that people will do it even at great cost, for the sheer sake of doing it.

The mark of a person who is in control of consciousness is the ability to focus attention at will, to be oblivious to distractions, to concentrate for as long as it takes to achieve a goal, and not longer."

Let's pull out the key points in Dr. Csikszentmihalyi description of the flow state.

According to Dr. Csikszentmihalyi, the flow state is when you have the ability to control your consciousness and focus your attention at will.

You are oblivious to any sort of distraction.

This allows you to concentrate for as long it takes to achieve what you've set out to do.

Would being able to incorporate these things into your daily life improve your productivity?

Not only that, flow is the state where nothing seems to matter except what you are doing in this moment.

You are completely focused on the task at hand, what's right in front of you.

Can you see how this could improve the enjoyment you get from work?

In the zone, nothing can distract you. Nothing can pull you away from your task. As a result, you are unstoppable. Nothing can keep you from making the progress you desire.

In the zone, your entire mind, body and spirit are occupied completely. There is no room for anything else.

You're focused, locked in, and completely engaged in what you're doing.

Distractions ping off you.

You're oblivious to what's happening around you.

When you're in flow state, your mind is 100% engaged.

You are completely and totally focused on what's in front of you. Rather than emptying your mind, you're trying to completely fill it with what you're doing.

You're highly attuned to what's in front of you.

This keeps you striving to hold your attention where you are.

You are so focused that nothing can distract you from the job in front of you. This is laser focus.

Would you like to be able to slip into the zone anytime you want?

You can!

In this book, you're going to learn techniques I've learned over the past 40 years or so. Techniques I've researched and used myself. Processes I've taught to people from all walks of life, of all ages and backgrounds to quickly slip into the zone and accomplish three times as much in half the time.

All this while developing a calm, focused and controlled mind.

My Path to Peak Performance

"The possession of anything begins in the mind."

— Bruce Lee

It was September 9, 1966, three days before my brother's 14th birthday, when a new TV show appeared on our living room television. I was 11 at that time, and my brother and I sat enthralled, watching Britt Reid, who was secretly the Green Hornet, and his sidekick Kato take on the bad guys. At the end of the show, we both agreed that Kato was much cooler than the Green Hornet and was probably the baddest dude we'd ever seen. Watching that episode of the Green Hornet was the start of my second great love.

Of course, Bruce Lee, who played Kato, went on to make some of the most iconic martial arts movies of all time. He is also a Hall of Fame Martial Artist and someone who affected the direction of the rest of my life and the lives of millions of other young people like me. Because of his influence, I, like thousands of others at the time, began studying martial arts, only instead of Kung Fu, like my idol Bruce Lee, I took judo at the local junior high school. Even though I never met him in person, Bruce Lee influenced me to make the study of martial arts a major part of my life. It was the beginning of my love affair with the study of the martial arts.

Humans - More Fascinating than Martial Arts?

While I love martial arts, I must confess that my first great love is the study of human behavior. You see, along the way, I've decided that human beings exhibit the most fascinating behaviors of any creature on earth.

My infatuation with human behavior began as a young boy when I started reading my mom's copies of "Guideposts," the magazine put out by the late Dr. Norman Vincent Peale, that extolled the power of positive thinking. I was truly fascinated by the stories inside those covers!

My fascination was the motivation behind me reading every book I could lay my hands on about psychology and human development during my six years in the Navy. It was behind my choice to change majors in college from engineering to psychology.

This fascination drove me to read literally thousands of books and articles about the many different facets of human behavior. I've been doing this regularly for the past 40 years or so.

Of all the facets of human behavior I studied, the one that piqued my curiosity most was that of performance. To be more specific, I wondered why some people seemed to be able to effortlessly accomplish anything they set out to do and some never even got out of the starting blocks.

This is where my two loves intersected. I found a subsection of martial arts students who always seemed to be able to perform at a very high level. This subsection were those martial artists who worked hard, persisted, and eventually earned their black belt.

Of course, there was a much larger subsection of martial arts students, the ones who never performed at such a high level. These were people who, for whatever reason, didn't believe they had what it takes.

The Truth About Black Belts

In the first weeks, or even in the first months of training, if you were to ask one hundred brand-new martial arts students, "What is your goal for training in the martial arts?" nearly all of them will answer, "I want to become a black belt."

While thousands of people begin studying the martial arts every year, only a very few actually go on to earn a black belt.

Why does this happen?

In my book *Secrets of the Black Belt Mindset*, I conclude this isn't because the people who earn a black belt have any special gifts or talents. No, there are many people who have superior physical talents who never go on to earn their black belt.

You can find these same phenomena in nearly any activity people attempt in life.

The reason some people earn their black belt is their mindset.

The people who go on to become black belts have learned to approach a problem or challenge differently. They look at problems not as unsurmountable obstacles, but rather as events to be learned from and then worked on from a different perspective, with a different approach.

Dr. Carol Dweck, the Stanford psychology professor, calls this the growth mindset. I call it the black belt mindset.

In *Secrets of the Black Belt Mindset*, I explain how a person can use certain processes and techniques to create a black belt mindset. These processes and techniques create what I call the habits of extraordinary success.

Understanding this mindset is the foundation for success. This is because a black belt mindset is one of the basic skills a person needs to move forward in life.

But, as any black belt will tell you, learning these skills is not enough. You need to be able to use them, at will, at any time and in any place.

This is what Mindful Mind Mastery is all about. The ability to converge the power of your mind, body and spirit in such a way that nothing can stand in your way. This comes from the ability to snap instantly into the peak performance zone, the place where nearly anything is possible. Where you, as Dr. Csikszentmihalyi so elegantly puts it, control your consciousness.

I call this convergence, the ability to converge your mind, body and spirit.

This is what you'll learn to do in this book.

Your Source, Your Psychology, and Your State

To access a peak performance state, you need three elements to converge for you:

- Your source
- Your psychology
- Your state.

In martial arts practice we call these elements mind, body, and spirit. While we're going to take a deep dive into each of these later, let's briefly examine each of them now.

Your Source

In the triad of mind, body and spirit, your source is mind.

Your mind contains the why behind what you do and think you want to do. You need to know your why to start the fire of desire. It is your motivation for success.

In this book you'll find processes that black belts and other peak performers use to uncover their motivation. This is how they successfully set up and achieve their goals.

While powerful, by itself your source can't create success. You also need to understand your psychology.

Your Psychology

Think of your psychology as the spirit needed to create success. As all high performers will attest, to achieve at your highest level, you must believe your stated outcome is possible.

It's understanding how the beliefs you hold about yourself affect you so you can control them.

For you to slip into a peak performance state, you must have beliefs that can generate the feeling, "I can do this!"

Your psychology contains all the beliefs you have about your abilities. It's the feeling inside that tells you whether or not you are able to do what you say you want to do.

Your beliefs breathe life into convergence.

How do you develop unshakable beliefs?

The same way a black belt or anyone who performs at a high level builds their beliefs. By mindfully calming the doubting voices in your head, the inner voices that interfere with your success.

In this book you'll learn a simple but powerful step by step process that you can use to turn down these voices.

You'll also learn powerful ways to replace those old voices with new empowering ones.

While calming those voices is essential, if your body isn't in the right state, when you try to do something difficult it will give you the message that you can't and you'll give up.

This is why harnessing the power of your state is so important.

Your State

Some people think that being a black belt is simply training the body. While the training the body is important, it's the last element of the convergence triad.

In this book, we'll refer to the feelings you generate from the way you hold your body, your physiology, as your state.

How you hold your body, or your state, gives you the confidence you need to reach a high level of performance.

In order to accomplish just about anything, you need to be able to transform your state from where you are now to operating at the highest level possible in the blink of an eye.

As any high-performing athlete, actor, or businessperson will tell you, your state, your posture, how you hold your body, sends feelings of confidence to your brain. To gain this confidence, you need to be able to know how to put your body into the most powerful state possible.

If you don't, your body tells you—and everybody around you—"I don't have what it takes to do this."

You build powerful physiology with good posture, proper breathing, and regular physical exercise.

In this book you'll discover specific processes black belts use to prepare their bodies for peak performance as well as to instantly transform themselves into a powerful state.

You Need All Three

To effortlessly slip into the zone, you need to know how to tap into your source, tune into your psychology, and transform your state. This is how you get your mind, body, and spirit ready to take the actions you need to succeed.

How to Use This Book

This book is broken into three sections: research and theory, exercises, and application.

In the first section, you'll learn about the theory as well as the research that has gone into the making of this book's philosophy.

While you may be tempted to bypass this section, my recommendation is to at least glance at the information.

Why?

Because understanding this information will boost your confidence in your ability to use it.

In the second section you'll find exercises.

In the martial arts, we have drills, or exercises, that develop basic skills. Through practice, these basic skills become automatic responses.

Like martial arts drills, practicing these exercises will help you develop the skills and responses you need to operate at a peak state.

The third section, Application, contain examples of how these processes have been applied in people's lives.

These are actions that people, just like you, have taken to get the results they wanted.

In the martial arts, beginning students model the examples set by their instructors and black belts. This is what helps them develop the habits of success.

Modeling is one of the processes all highly successful people use to take them to the top.

Having these models will do the same and for you.

Chapter 2

Creating a New Paradigm

"We don't see things as they are, we see them as we are."

— Anais Nin

It seems like every week there's a new book telling us that the way to peak performance, and ultimately success, involves doing this one amazingly powerful thing. The reason I know this is because I have invested in and read hundreds of these books, bought and listened to untold hours of these self-development programs and gone to or watched thousands of hours of self-improvement seminars.

Am I saying that I didn't receive any value from these books and programs?

No, not at all!

What I've found is, usually, each has a good method for generating a higher level of performance. The problem is these ideas, by themselves, don't result in first-rate, long-term, high quality results.

In addition to researching peak performance, I have also practiced and taught martial arts for a major portion of my life. What I've found is black belts can perform at a higher level than other students.

This isn't because they are special; it's because they have a different paradigm.

What the Heck is a Paradigm?

The first time paradigms were discussed were in Thomas Kuhn's book, *The Structure of Scientific Revolutions*.[1] In his book he explained that a paradigm simply helps you to organize the information you take in through your senses of touch, hearing, sight, taste, and smell.

Think about how much information you take in with your senses. In fact, right now, think about how the cloth of what you're wearing feels on your back.

Now, think about the feeling of the ground under your feet.

Until I mentioned them, you weren't even paying any attention to them. This is a good thing!

If you paid attention to them, and all the other sensory inputs you are getting right now, your brain would be overwhelmed.

To give these vast quantities of information meaning, and not drive yourself crazy, you need to be able to quickly summarize and categorize them. This distillation of information provides you with an input's meaning nearly instantaneously.

The reason this is important is it tells you how to respond in certain situations. It can also save your life.

What's Happening?

You hear a bark that sounds like a dog. You look to your left and see that the bark is coming from a golden retriever. You recognize the golden retriever as your neighbor's dog. Her tail is wagging playfully, and he looks like she's smiling at you.

You walk over to the dog and pat her on the head. She wags her tail even more and then saunters off, back to her own yard.

Now you hear a different bark. You look across the street and see that the bark is coming from a large pit bull.

You do not recognize this dog.

It's barking and snarling and baring its teeth while looking in your direction. You feel like he's looking straight at you. You slowly retreat into your house, lock the door, and call animal control.

While both were dogs, how you categorized and summarized the information you took in was what prompted you to take two vastly different actions. Your paradigm shaped your image of those two dogs, helping you make sense of what was happening and giving you a map that allowed you to navigate safely through your world.

A Map?

Do you remember what life was like before GPS?

If you were going someplace you were not familiar with, you would take a map with you. This allowed you to find where you were going.

While the map helped you find the right streets and get you to the right place, it didn't show you what the neighborhood actually looked like, as Google Maps does today. The map was merely a two-dimensional image of the area.

By definition, a map is a picture or representation of some part of the earth's surface. It shows us the relationship between, for example, a street's buildings to each other by distance, direction, and size.

What makes maps such a powerful tool, especially before cellphones, is that they are printed on a flat piece of paper. This makes them easy to carry around with us.

But, although they very are useful tools, what needs to be remembered is that a map is not a photograph, but rather a representation or a perspective of a part of the world.

Like a map, your brain has representations or perspectives about events you've experienced. As you gain new experiences, you also gain new perspectives.

These new perspectives expand the range of your mental maps. For example, let's say you have never tried broccoli because you were told as a child that it was "yucky." A new friend, whom you want to impress, invites you over and serves you broccoli.

You eye the broccoli suspiciously, but your friend assures you it's delicious.

You try it and find that you like it. A lightbulb goes off in your head.

Broccoli actually tastes good!

You have just discovered that your map was inaccurate. In turn, this causes your map or perspective about broccoli to change.

Unfortunately, most of the time we don't know when our maps aren't accurate or don't contain enough information.

Take the snarling pit bull we were talking about earlier.

After you went into the house, you peek out the window and witness it going after a rattlesnake you hadn't noticed in the corner of your yard. It bites and kills the rattlesnake, protecting you and making your neighborhood a safer place.

Then a man walks by and calls the dog's name. You watch as it trots over and rolls onto its back, allowing the man to rub its belly. This dog is not only a hero, he's also a lover.

The problem you had with the pit bull was your perspective was limited. You simply didn't have all the information you needed to make an accurate decision about the dog.

As a result, you organized the information you had coming into your senses about the dog incorrectly.

Of course, these inaccuracies happen to us all the time and not just with pit bulls. These incorrect perceptions affect how we think and feel about events occurring in our lives.

Unfortunately, an inaccurate perspective can, and often does, guide us in the wrong direction. To get on the peak performance path you need to know how to create a new or different paradigm—a mindful paradigm that black belts, and other peak performers, have learned to master.

The Mindful Paradigm

When presented with obstacles, instead of freaking out, black belts have learned to mindfully approach the challenge and stay in the moment.

Instead of pressing or overcompensating to try to out-muscle the problem, they calmly gather information. This allows them to evaluate the situation and respond to it appropriately.

Being able to respond appropriately keeps a black belt from overreacting. Instead of spiraling out of control in a critical situation, they stay calm, centered and in the moment.

They drop into the zone.

This gives them a calm awareness that allows them to see the situation clearly. Their clear perspective helps them to evaluate the information they receive accurately.

All of this is done in less than a blink of an eye.

How does this happen?

It comes from their ability to drop into the zone by aligning their source, psychology, and state.

In the zone time expands.

This allows them to deftly examine the information they are taking in and accurately compare it to their existing maps.

In this calm, mindful state, they make the right decision based on an accurate image. This image gives them the confidence that the actions they take will give them the outcome they desire.

Why are black belts able to do this so well?

For the same reason all peak performers are able to do this. The map that guides them has manifested itself through years of mindfully practicing martial arts. Through practice, and contemplation, they have developed a deep understanding of their why.

Their understanding of why they do what they do pushes everything else aside and guides them smoothly along their path in life.

Your why will do the same for you.

Martial arts practice has made the black belt examine his or her beliefs, the truths she or he holds about herself or himself. This understanding allows them to face and overcome the challenges and roadblocks that will stop others dead in their tracks.

Why are beliefs so important?

Because when you have taken the time to understand your beliefs, you can better accept who you are.

When you accept who you are, you can accept reality. You understand that you are responsible for how you got to where you are.

This acceptance of self-responsibility is liberating because old, false images of who you are can no longer hold you back. You understand that you are in control and you have the power to change what you want to change.

As you see yourself more clearly, you are able to embrace every part of you, the good and the not-so-good, This acceptance gives you the understanding that you can't improve what you don't allow yourself to see.

You are no longer blinding yourself to the truth.

With your eyes open, you can move confidently along your life's path.

This paradigm is your compass toward self-acceptance and personal growth. It guides you by removing the self-doubt that has, up until now, concealed your view. As you are able to see the world more accurately, you, like a black belt, are able to drop into the zone and operate in a peak performance state, whenever and wherever you want.

This is what gives you the power to do whatever it takes, in the only moment you have, right now, to get the outcome you want. This is why understanding and applying the mindful paradigm is so important.

By operating mindfully, you can get what you want out of life.

This is Not the Easy Button.

The black belt paradigm is not the easy button, but having said that, it doesn't mean learning this paradigm has to be difficult.

Like a good martial arts system, you can move through these processes the same way I moved through the martial arts.

The reason I was able to move from white belt, a beginner, to a fifth-degree master instructor is because I went through an easy-to-follow (notice I didn't say it was easy, only easy to follow), step-by-step system.

Like that martial arts system, this book lays out simple, easy to follow, step-by-step processes that will allow you to drop into the zone anytime or anywhere.

But it will take work!

As any successful martial arts student will tell you, you need to rehearse your techniques over and over and over again until they become automatic. This rehearsal is what gives you the ability to respond to an attack at the right time and with the right techniques automatically, without thinking.

The same goes for mindfully dropping into the zone. You will need to practice what you learn in this book over and over until you can use your techniques effortlessly and automatically.

Repetition is what allows black belts, world-class business leaders, actors, Olympic athletes, special forces operators and all those who perform at an extremely high level in any area of life to succeed where others don't.

They can use their paradigm to drop into the zone anytime and anywhere, without thinking.

The great news is that the practice isn't hard, and it doesn't have to take a lot of time. You just need to practice until the behavior you need for your desired outcome becomes your habitual response and, therefore, comes automatically.

It's that simple.

So, are you ready to start training?

If you are then let's begin!

PART I

Research and Theory

Introduction to Part I:

"There is an ecstasy that marks the summit of life, and beyond which life cannot rise. And such is the paradox of living, this ecstasy comes when one is most alive, and it comes as a complete forgetfulness that one is alive."

— Jack London

*H*ave you ever found yourself so immersed in a task that you completely lose track of time? When you finally look up from your task you discover that hours have passed by and it seems like you've just been working a couple of moments?

Do you recall how your focus was so intense that the world around you just faded away and the only thing that mattered at that moment was the task in front of you?

At this time, you were in a state of flow. This place is also known as the "zone."

The Flow Sate: AKA the Zone

"You have considerable power to construct self-helping thoughts, feelings and actions as well as to construct self-defeating behaviors. You have the ability, if you use it, to choose healthy instead of unhealthy thinking, feeling and acting."

— Albert Ellis

In the zone, you are totally immersed in what you are doing. This skyrockets your productivity. The world goes on around you, but you aren't distracted by it. This causes time to lose its meaning. Your tasks become deeply enjoyable and you find yourself stretching your abilities to reach an even higher level of performance, giving your life more meaning.

Being in flow brings all these benefits into the lives of those who learn to access it.

How can you access the flow state?

By using the elements of convergence.

Light My Fire

The three prerequisite ingredients needed for fire are fuel, oxygen, and heat. Put these three together in the correct quantities and they ignite.

The same is true for the three elements that make up convergence. Using convergence to drop into the zone means being able to tap into your source, tune into your psychology, and transform your state.

Tuning into this mindful state is how you can generate unstoppable focus and power.

These three elements aren't secret magical incantations from an ancient world. In fact, they aren't really secrets at all.

They are well-researched findings of modern social scientists who have studied human behavior with the sole purpose of documenting what works successfully for peak performers who consistently set, and accomplish, high levels of personal and professional achievement.

The great news is that the social scientists we're borrowing techniques from have used the scientific method to study human behavior. That means you and I can copy and then model their methods to achieve similar results.

That's exactly what you're going to learn to do.

We'll begin with your source.

Chapter 3

It All Begins with Why

"Make the WHY big enough — then the HOW and the WHEN will fall into place."

- Donny Epstein

*L*et's say you want to run a marathon, earn a million dollars a year, become a black belt, or study primate behavior.

While these goals are admirable, each one is going to take time and effort. Your goals are not going to happen by themselves.

This means you're going to have to do more than decide what you want. You need to work at accomplishing your goals.

But there are going to be times when sticking to your goals is hard. People, events and things will conspire against you, sapping your energy and motivation.

You just won't feel like working on them and you'll get stuck, unless.

Unless?

Unless you are deeply in touch with your why.

Without understanding your why, your goals are merely a checklist, simply a way to keep track of doing things that just aren't that hard.

Without Your Why Your Goals are Useless

It's a matter of choosing what is most important to you and putting that first. Once you have recognized your true purpose in life, this becomes much easier."

— Clarence Clemons

Setting a goal is easy.

Many people set goals all the time and, like all the martial arts students who set their goal to become a black belt, few people actually achieve them.

Why?

It's because while setting a goal is easy, it takes work to make your goal happen.

Sometimes (this should read always) when you're doing the work that needs to be done to achieve what you've set out to do, you run into roadblocks and adversity.

People, events and things will operate against you, sapping your energy and motivation. You just won't feel like working on your goal and you'll get stuck, unless...

Unless?

Unless you are deeply in touch with your why.

In order to continue working on your goals, no matter what difficulties you are facing, you must understand the source of your desire to achieve that goal.

How do you find your source?

By understanding why you get up in the morning.

The Goal-Seeking Species

We humans are goal-seeking by nature.

It's ingrained in our DNA.

Think about it like this. Every morning our ancestors needed to look for food, water, and a place to keep dry and warm to stay alive. They also needed to watch out for predators and competing human tribes.

They got up every morning knowing exactly why they did everything.

They hunted in certain areas because they knew there would be plenty of game there.

They kept safe by avoiding the hunting grounds of large predators like the saber-toothed tiger.

They knew the safest place to set camp.

They understood why they did every activity. This is why they survived and is why you are alive today.

These same needs drive our behaviors today.

While some drivers, like having food, water, and shelter, still help us to survive, other drivers, like financial success, athletic achievements, and getting that new position at work, come from a different source.

This is the source were going to look at next.

Why Do You Get Up in the Morning?

How do you discover your source? How do you uncover the deep desire behind what you want in life?

An easy way to begin thinking about your source is to answer the following question, *"Why do I get out of bed in the morning?"*

For Steve Jobs, it was his drive to make computers available to everyone.

For Jonas Salk, it was his drive to find the cure for polio.

For Marie Curie, it was her drive to research radioactivity.

For Elon Musk, it is his drive to bring humankind to Mars.

If someone were to ask any of them, "Why are you doing that?" they would be able to instantly respond with an answer. An answer that makes sense, at least to them, about moving them toward their desired result.

How can they do this?

They are able to do this because they had decided what they wanted and why.

So how can you figure out your source, your why, the reasons for going after your outcomes?

A good start would be to model what Steve Jobs did.

Do You Want to Keep Doing What You're Doing?

After being diagnosed with pancreatic cancer, Steve Jobs gave an amazing commencement speech. If you haven't already, find it on YouTube and listen to it.

In that speech he said, *"For the past 33 years, I have looked in the mirror every morning and asked myself: 'If today were the last day of my life, would I want to do what I am about to do today?' And whenever the answer has been 'No' for too many days in a row, I know I need to change something."*

How will you answer Steve's question?

If your answer is no, then it's time to uncover your why.

Chapter 4

You Only Have a Short Time

"Life is short, and every moment is precious."

—Gad Saad

In 1990, a movie titled *Short Time* came out. The movie is about a 50-year-old detective about to retire from the New York City Police Department. He has exactly eight days, in other words, a short time, until his retirement.

He's a divorced father of a ten-year-old son who lives with his estranged wife. He has strained relationships with both of them.

He tells himself that the biggest reason he wants to retire is to repair his relationship with his son by spending more time with him.

He doesn't want to be injured, or worse, with only eight days left on the force. All he wants to do is play it safe, so he spends his time looking for any way possible to stay away from any dangerous policing activities. In fact, he spends most of his time trying to avoid any work he possibly can.

All this changes when he goes to purchase a brand-new insurance policy.

To qualify for the new policy, he needs to take a physical. So, he and his partner go to the public employees' health clinic. Seated beside him is a bus driver who's scheduled for a random drug test.

Not realizing the two are detectives, the bus driver asks them, "If someone smoked marijuana two days ago, will it show up on their test?"

Flashing their badges, the two detectives simultaneously reply, "Yes!"

Seeing the badges, the startled bus driver then mutters, "I didn't say I used marijuana, I was just asking!"

As the bus driver steps to the other side of the clinic, the two detectives walk away, chuckling.

Since both the bus driver and the detective are giving urine samples, they end up in separate rooms directly across from each other. The cart holding the urine specimens is left, unguarded, in the hallway between the detective's and the bus driver's rooms. Not wanting to be busted for pot use, the bus driver sneaks out of his room and switches his urine sample with the detective's.

When the samples come back, the detective's blood sample, which is, of course, the bus driver's, shows he has a rare blood disease and will probably die within two weeks. It also shows that he has been smoking marijuana.

Of course, now the detective discovers he won't be able to take out his new insurance policy, but he also discovers that he has a very valuable insurance policy. An insurance policy with the police force. The only problem with this policy is he has to die on the job for his son to collect the payout.

The detective's attitude from changes someone who is just trying to get by to one who is giving his all. Instead of loafing, he throws himself into every dangerous situation he can to get himself killed.

Simultaneously, believing that he only has two weeks to live, the detective dives passionately back into a relationship with his ex- wife, his son, his partner, and everyone else he meets. Believing he is about to die, he wants to make the most of his "short time." He does everything he can to squeeze the most life possible out of his few remaining days.

Fortunately, the detective doesn't get himself killed. He also finds out about the urine sample switch but not until he's changed how he's living his life completely. His "brush with death" transformed him into a new man.

Here's the question.

Why did it take 50 years for him to figure out what was important to him?

You don't have to wait until time is short.

You can begin, right now, to figure out what motivates you, what is important and worthy of your time.

What If This Were Your Last Day on Earth?

After taking in the story about how the detective acted when he thought about having such a short time left, let's take another look at Steve Jobs' question, *"If today were the last day of my life, would I want to do what I am about to do today?"*

If your answer is no, that's great!

At least you know what you don't want.

This is a great start. Now you need to think about what you DO want.

Here's a technique I want to teach you right now.

It's called questioning.

Questions cause your mind to seek answers.

What's most important about this technique is that you ask yourself the right questions. Don't worry about this right now,

I'm going to give you the questions. We'll take a deep dive into how you can create the right kind of questions later.

For now, to get you thinking about what you do want, answer this question, *"If all the forces in the universe suddenly came together for me, what would I want my life to be like?"*

In the rest of this book, this will be referred to as the *"universe"* question and I promise it will be referred to again.

Now, before moving to the next step, find a notebook that you can use as a journal (we'll talk more about this in a while) and take three minutes to write down your response to this question. The reason you only have three minutes is this is just to get you started, not keep you from doing things to help you go after your goals.

(Go to https://tinyurl.com/Mindful-Mastery-Journal to get your FREE interactive journal especially designed for this book!)

This is your first exercise.

Don't skip it!

Now that you've answered that question (you did answer the question, didn't you?), to further expand your thinking, ask, *"If I were to win $10 million in the lottery, what would I do with my life?"*

Again, write your answer out in three minutes or less.

Do it now!

The Importance of Taking Action Now!

You purchased this book because you wanted to make some kind of change in your life. The only way this will happen is if you do the work.

These exercises will enable you to slip into the zone, quickly and seamlessly but only if you DO them!

So, make *"Do it now!"* your mantra when you see an exercise in this book.

For your outcome to become a real driver for you, you need to be able to answer these questions.

Why?

Because behavioral studies have found that all high-performing individuals can answer these questions every time they are asked, immediately, without hesitation. They perform at such a high level because they are motivated by the answers they have generated within themselves.

You will need to do this exercise every day until you too can answer these questions immediately, without hesitation.

If you don't take the time to do this exercise daily, you will continue to stay stuck in the place Steve Jobs was talking about!

Not putting in the effort to answer these questions, will cause you to come up with crappy answers like, "Oh, I don't know, I would just hope I could do lots of good things. You know, be my best."

What the heck does that mean? Your best compared to what?

You don't want to "be your best."

You want to operate at your peak. This will take the creation of goals—big, specific, extremely difficult goals.

This is how you put yourself in the zone.

Why do they need to be specific and difficult?

Because research shows that the more specific and difficult goals are, the more motivational they'll be. The problem with a vague outcome, like being your best, is it won't motivate you. It just can't motivate you.

To find the motivation you need to break out of your stuckness and get going on the path to your $10 million dollar goals, you have to be able to answer the question, *"Why do I get up in the morning?"*

You must understand the driving desire behind why you're doing what you're doing. You need to know your why, your source.

Understanding and harnessing your why is absolutely essential to being able to drop into the zone.

This is why you need to work on uncovering your source.

If your source is not in alignment with your goals, you'll remain stuck in place, unable to move forward toward the life you desire.

Without your why you are just spinning your wheels. You can't drop into the zone of something you aren't 100 percent invested in.

As a result, you'll flounder and become disenchanted and quit. That's not what you want.

You want something more for your life.

This is why you need to choose something that you feel is worthy of you and that challenges you. Something to drive you to get up in the morning.

Does it Make You Happy?

Another key element of understanding your source is your why needs to make you happy. This is because happiness is motivating.

Now, this isn't the kind of happiness you feel when you close the big deal, buy the big house, or drive that brand-new car the first time.

That type of happiness doesn't last.

Why?

Because that kind of happiness is a result of something outside of you, extrinsic events. These never last.

This is the type of happiness you feel when you spend time with that special someone, experience a new level of personal growth, or help someone who cannot return the favor.

It that special kind of happiness you feel whenever you just think about it. Whatever "it" happens to be.

So how can you discover this type of happiness? By understanding your deep, intrinsic motivators.

Chapter 5

Inside or Outside?

"One can not reflect in streaming water. Only those who know internal peace can give it to others."

—Lao Tzu

W here does your motivation come from? Social scientists tell us that motivation to act can either come from inside or outside ourselves. Psychologists call motivation from inside us *intrinsic*, and motivation from outside ourselves, *extrinsic*.

In the book *Why We Do What We Do*² Edward L. Deci tells us about research done by Richard Ryan and Tim Kasser, who focused on six types of life aspirations. Three were intrinsic and three were extrinsic.

The three extrinsic aspirations were being wealthy, being famous and being physically attractive. The three intrinsic aspirations were the psychological needs for competence, relatedness, and autonomy.

While they found that both extrinsic and intrinsic goals could be motivating, those aspirations that are intrinsic are satisfying by themselves. In other words, they make us happy.

Intrinsic Motivation

You are intrinsically motivated when you are engaged in a behavior because you find it personally rewarding, or you feel happy just because you're doing it, because you *want* to do it. When doing something just because you want to do it, often you will find yourself unaware of how much time is passing. You can miss meals as you focus on the tasks at hand.

As we've already discussed, this is flow state, being in the zone. In the zone, you feel like you're in another world, a world where no one or nothing can disturb or upset you.

You are overflowing with true happiness.

Extrinsic Motivation

Extrinsic motivation is being motivated by a reward or punishment, something that comes from outside of you. This is why you do a last-minute report over the weekend, to be recognized for your efforts and/or so your boss won't fire you.

But extrinsic motivation is also when you are pursuing a goal simply to gain fame or fortune. While there is nothing wrong with achieving these as by-products of accomplishing your outcomes, the pursuit of fame or fortune doesn't come from inside of you. It isn't intrinsic.

As Ryan and Kasser point out, these types of extrinsic goals *"bring our attention to what we have, rather than what we are."* By themselves, these goals won't make you happy.

So how do you uncover your intrinsic motivation? You do this by understanding how to satisfy your basic human psychological needs. This is where the self-determination theory comes in.

The Self-Determination Theory

"Each man is questioned by life; and he can only answer to life by answering for his own life; to life he can only respond by being responsible."

—Viktor E. Frankl

There are literally dozens of ideas and theories about human psychological needs. Each attempts to explain how we humans acquire our feelings of psychological well-being.

People have been curious about these needs for thousands of years. It probably won't surprise you that this search has resulted in an extremely wide range of psychological theories.

While some of these theories are long and complex and others are short and sweet, social scientists have generally come to agree on one set of needs. Edward Deci and Richard Ryan describe these needs in the Self -Determination Theory.[3]

In their theory, Deci and Ryan argue that our three basic psychological needs are relatedness, competence, and autonomy. When these needs are met, you have a feeling of well-being. Knowing how to meet these needs is essential to understanding your source.

Let's take a quick look at each of them.

Relatedness

Relatedness is about the need to have close connections with other humans. Deci describes this as *"a need to create and cultivate close friendships and intimate relationships, a need to love and be loved."*[4]

This is the essence of relatedness.

The drive to be connected with others.

This need for connection is why we join martial arts schools, charitable organizations, sports teams, gardening, or Rotary Club. It's also why Facebook and other social media sites are so attractive.

They all allow us to connect and bond (even superficially, as in the case of so many social media sites) with other people.

All humans need to have close connections.

Without them, we can become mentally unstable. In fact, psychologists will tell you that isolated people are much more susceptible to depression and mental illness. Medical doctors will tell you that they are more susceptible to illnesses of all sorts.

Evolutionary psychologists take this a step further, arguing that our need to connect is genetic, at our very core. Our need for relatedness is the result of needing the group for our survival.

This is because, on the savanna, your ancestors were constantly being exposed to potentially fatal dangers, such as animal predators and tribes of competing humanoids. Unless you were in a group, you wouldn't survive.

So, to have a healthy sense of psychological well-being, you must feel connected (not just superficially) to other people. Without this connection, you expose yourself to dangers just as potentially fatal as a saber-toothed tiger attack.

Competence

We also have a need to be able to manipulate things in our environment in a way that gets us what we want.

This is the definition of competence.

There are many ways to be able to get what you want out of your environment. People derive competence from a variety of means.

For example, you can be physically competent. This includes being good in a sport like tennis or a physical activity such as the martial arts.

You can be intellectually competent. This can be the feeling of competence in a school subject such as philosophy, finance, or psychology.

You can be emotionally competent. You can get what you want by your ability to work well with other people and getting the most out of your friendships.

You can also be artistically competent. Perhaps you are an excellent cellist or sculptor.

You can derive competence from nearly anything. The list is endless.

You get feelings of competence when you attempt to achieve complex goals. These can be goals like learning a new language, taking martial arts classes, writing a book, completing a self-development course, or learning how to draw well enough that people can tell what you drew without asking.

As you continue to try, progress and persist, you grow your feelings of competence. This is because, as you go through this process, you are learning that your actions can control your environment.

This feedback process develops your feelings of positive psychological well-being.

Autonomy

Autonomy is the final of your three basic psychological needs.

It is being able to choose where you put your time and effort. It's the feeling of freedom you receive when you are able to decide what you want to do and how you go about doing it.

According to Deci, autonomy is "acting in accordance to one's self, in charge of one's own actions and being authentic."

Another way to look at autonomy is when you are totally and completely self-motivated.

Think about it like this. You are self-motivated when you choose your behaviors because of your intrinsic values. It is just the opposite of being controlled by people and things in the outside world.

You do more when you are guided internally You work at a higher level, you function smoothly.

This feeling of autonomy helps to drive you into a state of flow, into the zone. This is the place where you find greater creativity, increased personal responsibility, healthy behaviors and lasting change.

Autonomy- self-motivation—is at the heart of peak performance.

Chapter 6

It's Time to Wake Up!

"The ultimate value of life depends upon awareness and the power of contemplation rather than upon mere survival."

—Aristotle

T he things that give you feelings of relatedness, competence, and autonomy, are the things that can help you
find your source. They will absolutely help you answer
the question, *"Why do I get out of bed in the morning?"*

The problem many people face is that they simply aren't aware
of what's most important to them. They go through life focusing
on things that don't matter.

They are sleepwalking through life.

The Devil Made Me Do It!

When I was a kid, one of the most popular shows on television was
The Ed Sullivan Show. Since it was a variety show, Ed would bring
on all types of entertainers, including comedians.

Flip Wilson was one of my favorites. One line that he said
became quite popular.

When Flip was asked why he did something that wasn't quite right, he would reply, "The devil made me do it!"

In other words, he did it because he had no idea of what he was doing. Social scientists call this a lack of awareness.

Awareness is the ability to recognize what you are doing, while you are doing it. Because you recognize what you're doing you also either know or can figure out WHY you are doing it.

For awareness to work, you must be present. You have to be paying attention to be aware.

Unfortunately, most people walk around in a kind of sleepwalking daze, having no idea what they are doing.

Right now, you might be asking, "Is he saying that the devil really made me do it? Am I possessed, acting like some kind of zombie?"

The simple answer to this is, "Well, yes!"

Let's take a look at why.

Your Two Separate (and Unequal) Minds

Some neuroscientists, and most psychologists, tell us that although we have one brain, we have two minds: the conscious and the unconscious (also known as the subconscious) minds.

The conscious mind controls our surface behaviors and the unconscious controls all our other behaviors.

I prefer to use the term "other-than-conscious processes" for our second mind, because it oversees all those other processes below the surface, including those of the autonomic nervous system.

Your conscious mind oversees logic and reason. It's the part of the mind that we believe is in control, but it isn't.

If your conscious mind were in control, you could change any behavior any time you wanted, and you could do it as easily as deciding to put on a different pair of shoes.

But you can't.

Your mind just doesn't work that way.

Why?

It's because your conscious mind isn't in control. Like we already discovered, it's your subconscious mind that is taking in all your sensory information, working with your lizard brain to keep you safe.

While your other-than-conscious processes keep you safe, they also are why you often find yourself doing things that you know aren't good for you. Things like reaching for a sugary snack or yelling at your significant other or a coworker.

They are baked-in behaviors you don't realize are going to happen, until it's too late. You do these things before you realize that you're doing them.

When you do these things, it's like there's a different person living inside of you, the real you and a zombie.

While this might alarm you, I want to assure you that you don't need to look for an exorcist. You actually need your zombie mind, or other-than-conscious processes. They are essential for your survival.

They work like the operating system of your computer—out of sight and in the background. Like a computer's operating system, you need them to function correctly.

You see your other-than-conscious processes operate many of the physical functions beneath your normal level of waking consciousness. Things like blinking your eyes, digesting your food, regulating your heartbeat, and breathing.

These are processes you are very rarely ware of unless something goes wrong with them. In fact, this is the only time anyone pays attention to them.

The fact is you don't think, or even want to think, about these processes.

Your other-than-conscious processes also control your habits, those things you do automatically, and thus, most of your behaviors. This is why it can seem like you are acting like a zombie, because you are.

How Do Our Habits Make Us Zombies?

"It is psychological law that whatever we desire to accomplish we must impress upon the subjective or subconscious mind."

—Orison Swett Marden

While you might think your conscious mind is in charge, it's your other-than-conscious processes that control nearly everything you do. These processes control most of your behaviors.

Don't believe me?

Do this exercise.

Cross your arms.

Note whether your right or left arm is on top.

Now switch your arms.

If your right arm was on top put your left arm on top, or vice versa.

How does that feel to you?

Weird, right?

Why does it feel weird?

It's because your zombie mind doesn't like change. You feel weird because your zombie-like processes are used to whatever arm you had on top first.

When you switched, your subconscious started screaming, "You've got the wrong arm on top, dummy!"

If this doesn't convince you, the next time you put on a pair of socks, note which sock you put on first.

Write down what sock you put on first on a sticky note.

Put that sticky note by where you usually put on your socks, so you can see it the next time you put them on.

Now when you get dressed, put the other foot's sock on first. How does that feel to you?

Probably as weird as when you reversed how you crossed your arms.

Why does it feel so weird?

It's because your other-than-conscious processes have already decided which sock should go on first. Your zombie processes have taken over your thinking.

There is good news, though. By realizing you have these habitual behaviors, you have begun to wake up.

You are becoming aware.

Awareness is the first step in zombie recovery.

Chapter 7

Birth of Your Zombie

"If our subconscious was attractive, we wouldn't have to bury it down deep within us"

—Douglas Coupland

A wealthy businessperson was worried about her son's bad habits. She decided to seek counsel from a wise, old man. The old man met the woman's son and took him out for a stroll.

They walked into the woods, and the old man showed the boy a small sapling and asked him to pull it out of the ground. Easily, the boy did so, and they walked on.

The old man then asked the boy to pull out a small plant. The boy did that with little effort also. As they walked along, the old man asked the boy to pull out a small bush.

Again, the boy did it easily.

Next, the old man pointed out a small tree. The child struggled but was finally was able to pull it from the ground.

Finally, the old man showed him a bigger tree and asked the child to pull it out of the ground. The boy struggled mightily but failed several times.

The old man had him stop and they sat down together. Smiling, he said, "The is the same with habits, good or bad. They are easy to remove when they are small, nearly impossible once they have grown and become part of our life."

Zombie Origins

Like the boy, you may have developed some habits that you struggle with. Let's take a quick look at how these habits are shaped.

Today it might seem that putting on your right sock first or putting your left leg in your pants first is "natural," but is it really?

Of course, it's not.

These behaviors are not natural, you had to learn them the same way you learned nearly all of your other behaviors. When you first learned these behaviors as a child, you had to think about them. Putting on clothes took thought the same as almost everything else you did.

Where did these behaviors come from?

Your parents or caretakers taught you some of these behaviors, for example, how to put on your socks or pants. These same people showed you how to brush your teeth and tie your shoes.

When you started learning how to do these tasks, your parents, or whoever taught you how to do these activities, spent a lot of time helping you.

But after a while, you got the hang of it. They didn't have to help you anymore because you could do them by yourself. You could do them yourself because you didn't have to think about how you did them anymore.

Accomplishing these tasks became part of your other-than-conscious processes, and you are much better because of it. This is because your other-than-conscious processes are saving you lots of time and energy.

Just think how difficult your life would be if, each time you tied your shoes, you had to think, "Okay, now I've got to loop-the-loop and, what's next now?" or if you had to think about how to slip your arm into your shirt or blouse.

You wouldn't accomplish much if you had to think about doing these routine tasks all the time, would you?

The same goes for tasks that aren't so routine, or at least shouldn't be as routine. Tasks where you should actually be paying attention.

You know—tasks like driving.

Learning to Drive

Think back to when you began learning how to drive. Can you remember what that was like?

When you first start driving, there is so much to think about. When you get into the car, you have to adjust the mirrors and the seat. As you drive, you have to be aware of pedestrians, other cars, stop signs, and so much more.

When you are learning to drive, you have to THINK a lot.

You have to learn how much pressure your foot needs to use to brake properly, so the car doesn't stop with a jerk or crash into another car.

If you learn to drive a car with a clutch, it can be overwhelming. In fact, when I first began learning how to drive with a clutch in an old VW bug, I hit the gas instead of the brake and drove it up over the curb. This is probably why they used VW bugs to teach drivers education back in the day.

Even though it took a lot of effort at first, it wasn't long before you could drive with one arm out the window, one hand on the wheel, all while intermittently sipping a soft drink. If a car pulled out in front of you, instead of thinking what to do, you applied the brakes quickly and easily and then followed it up by honking the horn and shouting obscenities.

Well, maybe you don't yell obscenities, but it was a one of the things I learned to do along the way.

I'm still working on this one.

The point is you know how to put the right pressure on the brakes at just the right time. You have developed the habit of knowing how to brake properly. You have it deeply ingrained into your other-than-conscious processes.

You do this behavior automatically.

In fact, this habit is so ingrained in your other-than-conscious processes that if you're riding in the passenger seat of a car next to your spouse or a friend and a car pulls out in front of you, where does your foot go?

More than likely, it pushes down on the carpet on the floor-board where the brake would be if you were in the driver's seat.

You've done this, haven't you?

Of course you have, we all do it!

Why do you press on the imaginary brake pedal even though you are consciously aware that pressing your foot on the floor will not stop the car?

It's because your other-than-conscious processes took over, leaving you with a cramped foot and the carpet with a deep shoe impression.

You just couldn't help yourself.

The devil made you do it.

Your inner zombie took over.

So how can you control your inner zombie?

We'll take a deep dive into this in Chapter 23.

Chapter 8

All You Need is Love

"All you need is love."

—John Lennon

In chapter 5, you discovered the three is basic psychological needs. These, as you recall, they are competence, autonomy and relatedness.

In this chapter, we're going to take a deeper dive into relatedness, which is what the Beatles song title above is all about: our need to love and be loved.

As humans, we have a deep desire to connect with other people. We go through our lives creating and cultivating close friendships and intimate relationships. As a result, this can become a large driver of your why.

Most people spend a large portion of their life trying to connect with others. It's also why some people become peak performers. For some, it's even why they choose to put in the time and energy needed to earn a black belt.

I began taking Tang Soo Do (Korean Karate) lessons as an adult because I thought I wanted to be the next Chuck Norris.

Along with Bruce Lee, I thought Norris was one of the coolest people in the world and, on top of that, they were movie stars.

I figured if I learned how to kick and punch like they did, maybe I could become rich and famous too! While I began training in Tang Soo Do for other reasons also, I must confess that, in the beginning, this was my biggest fantasy.

As I have aged, I have very stiff hips. This meant that to develop any kind of kicking ability, I had to work very hard to improve my hip's flexibility.

To improve, I would stretch every morning and every night. While my flexibility did improve quite a bit, to this day, compared with most people who practice a kicking martial art, my hips are stiff and tight.

While I did have stiffness issues, one of the things that has set me apart my whole life has been persistence. Some who know me well would call it bull-headedness.

At times, my hips were so sore that I had to take ibuprofen to walk. This made me think about giving up, but I didn't.

Why did I keep going?

Well, part of it was because of a quality now known as grit. Grit is a term Professor Angela Duckworth from the University of Pennsylvania coined for stick-to-it-ness.[1]

But it was more than just that. It also had a lot to do with the fact that I was enjoying the camaraderie of my fellow students and the attention I was receiving from the instructors and black belts.

I began taking classes in what is now my hometown, San Diego. I had grown up on the coast in Central California in Seaside and after I left the Navy, I only had a very tiny circle of friends.

---

[1] Duckworth, Angela (2016). Grit: The Power of Passion and Perseverance. Scribner.

As my fellow martial arts fanatics got to know me better and accepted me, I felt good about myself. These fellow martial artists were filling my need for relatedness.

You have this need, too.

You also have goals motivated by relatedness, the need to love and be loved. To figure out if this is the primary driver of something you're attempting to accomplish, you simply need to think about the words you're attaching to it.

Words that describe this need are family, friends, community, teamwork, making a difference, and service. I'm sure you can think of many others.

What they all have in common is the need to bond deeply with others.

If you are doing something that applies to these values, then the need you are fulfilling is connecting or relatedness. You are doing it out of your need to love and be loved.

Chapter 9

Command Central

"We can let circumstances rule us, or we can take charge and rule our lives from within."

—Earl Nightingale

In the movie *White House Down* (and all the other movies of this genre), after the White House is attacked, the political and military leaders of the United States all gather at "command central," a place where they can take in pertinent information and then control the action necessary to retake the White House and, ultimately, keep the world safe.

While you probably won't ever be expected to save the world from nuclear destruction, you do have a need to feel like you are in charge of getting the results you want. The larger the portion of outcomes you feel you have control of, the more your need for competence is filled.

Like the actions of the hero in *White House Down*, peak performers will go to extreme lengths to fill their need for competence, to feel they are in control of their lives.

Olympic athletes will train for hours every day for years upon years, just to have the opportunity to compete in one race or be part of a single Olympic event.

Scholars and researchers will study a tiny slice of a subject, sometimes for many decades, to become competent in their own eyes and the eyes of their peers.

Martial arts students will train for years and years simply to have the opportunity to test for and hopefully earn their black belt.

These peak performers all have one thing in common: the need to feel competent, to get the things they want out of their environment. They have a strong desire for competence.

How can you determine if competence is the primary driver of an outcome?

Again, decide which words you attach to it.

Words that come to mind are accomplishment, prosperity, excellence, knowledge, work, credibility, professionalism, and discipline. I'm sure you can think of others.

If you are pursuing something that relates to these values, then the need you are fulfilling is that of competence. You have a deep desire to feel that you are good at what you are doing.

It's the feeling of control you get from doing something well that feeds this need.

Chapter 10

Let Me Do it Myself!

"The most common way people give up their power is by thinking they don't have any."

—Alice Walker

f you have raised kids, you've probably heard the words, "Let me do it myself!"

In fact, I'll bet that when you were very young, these words might have even escaped your own lips. I'd almost guarantee it.

How can I make such a pronouncement?

Because the final of our three basic psychological needs, autonomy, is at our very core.

It's a need that's so important that, when we can't fill it, it can cause death.

You might be thinking, "It can cause death, no way!"

Yes way, and there is scientific research to back this up.

While many studies on autonomy focus on children, a 1970s study focused on the elderly. Ellen Langer and Judy Rodin conducted a study of elderly residents in nursing homes to find out what kind of impact autonomy could have on them.[5]

Their theory was that older people in nursing facilities deteriorated rapidly, both mentally and physically, because they lived in a "decision free" environment. In other words, they lacked a feeling of autonomy.

They found all decisions were being made in these homes were by the facility and none by the residents. Decisions about the tidiness and layout of their rooms, how they spent their leisure time, what they ate for their meals, and even their grooming was scheduled and executed came without the input of the residents.

The two researchers designed a simple intervention where a portion of the residents were called together for a meeting. The chief administrator explained that they were free to make some of the decisions that the staff had previously made for them.

They were told they could decide how they spent their free time, how they groomed themselves, the way they arranged their rooms, and anything else that came to their minds. They were also given the option to care for a plant by themselves, without help from the staff.

The contrasting group were given essentially the same options, but, instead of being free to choose what they wanted, they were told that they had permission to do these activities. In other words, they were being given permission to decide how they spent their free time, groom themselves, or arrange their rooms. While the language distinction is subtle, the difference in results between the two groups were startling, as you'll see in a moment.

Additionally, instead of caring for the plant themselves, the non-choice resident group's plants would be cared for by the nursing staff.

An example of the communication to the choice group was, "Let us know what you want to change."

On the other hand, the permission group was told, "Let us know how we can help you."

The differences were astounding.

Those in the choice group reported feeling happier and were more active compared to the permission group. They rated their nurses higher, were more mentally, and physically, alert.

This was just the opposite for the permission group. During the experiment, the non-choice group's mental and physical health actually deteriorated.

The most alarming of the results was that while 15 percent of the choice group died within 18 months, 30 percent of the non-choice group died within the same period. The lack of choice doubled a resident's chance of dying.

What we can learn from these results is free choice greatly impacts our contentment and feelings of happiness. It gives us a reason for living.

On the other hand, the lack of autonomy can actually kill us.

How do you know if autonomy is driving your outcome? Words that describe a need for autonomy are financial independence, personal growth, personal choice, and adventure. As with the other values, there are many more to choose from.

If you are pursuing something that relates to these values, then the need you are fulfilling is that of autonomy. You have a deep desire to experience that feeling of freedom you get when you are able to decide what you want to do and how you do it.

You want to do it yourself.

Chapter 11

So What's Your Source?

"The only person you are destined to become is the person you decide to be."

—Ralph Waldo Emerson

As we've discovered, the source behind your quest for an outcome is a result of fulfilling one of the Self-Determination Theory's three basic needs. As a reminder the three needs are:

- Competence
- Autonomy
- Relatedness

Does this mean that an outcome has only one need as its source?

Of course not.

These needs can, and probably should, overlap.

What you need to keep in mind is that you have each of these needs. Understanding how they drive you will help you utilize them to operate at a peak state.

This is what you want to do, right?

This is why you need to figure out where your source comes from.

But, before we talk about how to better identify what's driving you, let's examine the next element of convergence—your psychology.

Chapter 12

I Think I Can!

"As you think, so shall you become."

—Bruce Lee

D o you remember the children's story, *The Little Engine That Could?*

Let's refresh your memory.

Watty Piper wrote *The Little Engine That Could* way back in 1930, and it has been a staple for children, at least in the U.S.A., ever since.

In case you have forgotten, the book is about a train that needs to bring toys and food to good children on the other side of a large mountain, but before they could be delivered, the train engine broke down.

Other bigger engines came by, and the broken engine asked each one if they would help pull the train over the mountain. One by one, for different reasons, they turned her down, until finally she asked a very little engine that happened by for help.

The engine was very small and had only worked in the train station, so she had never been over the mountain, but she understood that the good children would be depending on her to get the toys and food. So she hitched the other train behind her and started on her way, saying, "I think I can, I think I can, I think I can!" as she moved along.

As she struggled up the mountainside, she continued to say, "I think I can" to herself, over and over, until she reached the peak. Then, with a sigh of relief, she said, "I thought I could, I thought I could, I thought I could," all the way down to deliver the toys and food to the good children below.

At a very early age, that little engine was teaching us about beliefs, telling us that all we had to do was believe and we could achieve whatever it was we wanted.

But is that really true?

Do you always achieve everything you believe?

The Psychology of Your Beliefs

Your beliefs help or hinder what you think is possible.

They do this by giving you a reference, or framework, for your experiences.

How you frame an experience gives it significance. Something that you frame as important or significant will stay available for quick retrieval in your zombie mind for a long time.

This is why you can still remember what you think your parents or teachers told you long into adulthood. It's also why that memory can still affect what you think or believe about yourself today.

What you need to keep in mind is that significant beliefs can push you forward, or hold you back.

Death Sentence

"When we know better, we do better."

—Maya Angelou

Beliefs are powerful. Just like the little engine that could, there are countless stories of people who have been driven to success because they believed they could. There are also just as many stories about people who have been held back because of their beliefs.

For example, a woman who believes her illness is incurable will begin to organize her life and actions around that belief. The doctors have given her the fatal diagnosis and she believes it's too late.

She believes there's nothing that can be done.

She resigns herself to what the doctor told her and makes many, nearly inconspicuous and often subconscious, decisions that fall in line with those beliefs. While she doesn't consciously try to make her situation worse, her subconscious guides her in the direction of her beliefs.

The result?

This woman died in exactly when the doctors predicted she would.

Another woman deeply believes that her illness can be cured. She makes contrasting decisions, defying the doctor's prediction. This woman's behavior is also guided by her beliefs.

Like the other woman, she makes many decisions, again nearly imperceptible, that move her in the direction of her beliefs. For this woman, the time window of the death sentence passes and she watches it disappear into the past as she lives on.

While there is no assurance that one of these women will survive and the other won't, doctors and social scientists agree that the woman with the optimistic outlook, the one who believed she could be cured, has a much higher probability of being cured.

One woman died, the other lived. This is how your beliefs can become a death sentence.

Breakthrough Beliefs

"Boards don't hit back."

– Bruce Lee
as "Mr. Lee" in Enter the Dragon (1973)

One personal illustration I like to use about beliefs comes from decades of martial arts training, specifically breaking boards. Board breaking is part of belt rank tests in many martial arts systems. Most, perhaps as many as 95 to 98 percent, of the students who attempt to break boards do so on their first try.

But there are always a few that don't.

When the student doesn't break the board on his first try, he will try again. Only on the second try, he does even worse.

Each additional try becomes feebler, and the student struggles to maintain his composure. Often after only three or four misses, he gives in. As a result, the board robs him of the outcome he said he so deeply desired.

So, the question always is, "Why didn't this student break the board?"

In every one of these cases, the reason they didn't break the board wasn't because of their strength or ability.

-I can state this with certainty because I have seen children as young as five years old break a board; I have seen people who are going through chemotherapy break the board; I have seen 80-year old students break the board.

So, what's holding the non-board-breakers back?

While sometimes it's because a student is so hyped up they can't focus properly, nearly 99 percent of the time it's because he had doubts about whether he could break the board in the first place. His beliefs about being able to break the board held him back from getting to his desired outcome.

On the other hand, a successful board breaker believes she can break the board. She has seen others break the board, so she knows it is possible.

Her instructors have repeatedly told that she can break the board. As a result, she deeply believes she can break the board. Her psychology is in the right place.

Her psychology and her beliefs were what gave her the concentrated power that a non-board-breaker lacks. This allows her to easily accomplish what she has set out to do.

Just like a successful board breaker, your beliefs are what help you shape your results.

So, like *The Little Engine That Could* told us, what you believe you can do, you can achieve.

Yet, time after time, we don't achieve.

Does this mean we simply don't believe enough?

And if we don't believe enough, how can we align our beliefs with our goals in a way that allows us to do what's needed to achieve them?

Before we look at these answers, let's examine where our beliefs come from.

Parents, Siblings, Teachers, and Peers

"We all have our own life to pursue, our own kind of dream to be weaving, and we all have the power to make wishes come true, as long as we keep believing."

—Louisa May Alcott

How we learn to fit into society, or as social scientists put it, our socialization, greatly affects our beliefs. As children, we learn the values of our culture through experiences in our homes, schools, places of worship, and neighborhoods and what behaviors are in alignment with our culture. These behaviors are called societal norms.

We get feedback from our parents, peers, and teachers, about what behaviors are acceptable, or "normal." The problem with this feedback is that it often limits what we think we can and cannot do. While I believe that nearly all parents and teachers sincerely want to help us grow into everything we can become, their beliefs can greatly affect how we perform.

A famous social science example comes from an experiment performed in 1964 by Harvard professor Robert Rosenthal at an elementary school south of San Francisco.[6] In the experiment, Rosenthal tweaked a normal IQ test and told the teachers that this special "new" test could predict which kids were about to experience a dramatic improvement in their IQ.

In other words, the test predicted which kids would become "special."

After the children took the test, Rosenthal randomly chose several children from every class, and declared they were predicted to have high IQs. In reality, there was nothing at all different about these kids from the rest. What was different was the teacher's beliefs that these kids were going to bloom intellectually during the school year.

For the next two years, Rosenthal followed these children. What he found was the teachers' expectations of these kids really did affect the students' IQ.

In fact, in his report he wrote, "If teachers had been led to expect greater gains in IQ, then increasingly, those kids gained more IQ."

The teachers' feedback to these children made a huge difference on their performance. They believed that the students were special and they became special.

This is how powerfully feedback from significant people can affect our abilities.

Your parents' and teachers' expectations of you, along with feedback from your peers, helped you to form your beliefs about yourself. This feedback let you know what your capabilities were or were not and you carried these beliefs into adulthood.

If you answered a math question correctly, you learned that you were "smart" in math by your teacher's approval. If you went with your parents to visit their friends at two years old and you hung to your mom's leg for protection, your parents saying, "Oh, she's shy," taught you that you are shy.

If you answered a reading question incorrectly and the class giggled, you learned from your peers' feedback that you weren't smart enough to volunteer answers in class. On the playground, if you were selected first for a team, you learned that you were "good at sports," while if you were the last one picked you learned just the opposite

Through the feedback from your parents, teachers, and peers, you learned whether you were smart, athletic, outgoing and so on, or not. These responses to you are what make up your beliefs and they are all stored up in your zombie mind.

Chapter 13

Beliefs and the Zombie Mind

"When I was a boy, I always saw myself as a hero in comic books and in movies. I grew up believing this dream."

—Elvis Presley

Susan Butcher won the 1986 Alaskan Iditarod, the grueling 1,158-mile sled dog race from Anchorage to Nome. She tells a story about being in second place one year and, when she found there was no way she could win, she vowed, "Next year I'll win."

She went home and trained intensively.

The next year she gained the lead. Near the end of the race, however, another driver had overtaken her, and Susan felt she was too tired to hold the lead.

Talking to her dogs, she promised, "Well, next time we'll win."

Listening to herself, she was struck with the thought "No one wins this time who plans to win next time!"

With this she called on everything within herself for one last burst of speed. Susan passed the leader and won her first Iditarod. After this, she became a four-time winner of that exhausting race.

How did Susan Butcher win that race?

She believed she could.

Growth or Fixed?

By now, you're saying, "Okay," I get it. We get our beliefs as kids. Does this mean my beliefs are hammered in stone? Can I change my zombie mind's beliefs?"

The answer is, it depends.

What does it depend on?

It depends on your mindset.

Stanford psychologist Carol Dweck has performed decades of research on a concept she calls mindset. In her book *Mindset: The New Psychology of Success*,[2] she argues that it's not just our abilities and talent that bring us success—it's the mindset we approach them with.

She defines these as either a fixed or a growth mindset.

Professor Dweck defines a fixed mindset as one that believes we have a fixed amount of an ability, such as for volleyball or math. This mindset leads us to believe that we succeed, or fail, based on the amount of this fixed or limited resource.

So, if you happen to be born with a great deal of "math intelligence," you'll do well at math.

But if you're not?

Well, don't think about growing up to be a mechanical engineer.

On the other hand, some people have a growth mindset. This is the mindset that our abilities are like Play-Doh. We mold and shape our abilities as we play with them.

As we play with our abilities, we become better at them.

My belief is that nearly all black belts fall into the growth category. This is because, although some people bring more raw

---

[2] Ballantine Books, 2007.

talent to the table than others, every black belt must constantly learn how to improve their skills. If they didn't believe they had the ability to improve their skills, they would just give up.

But as Professor Dweck's research points out, this is true for everything.

A Winner's Mindset

> *"We can't have full knowledge all at once. We must start by believing; then afterwards we may be led on to master the evidence for ourselves."*

—Thomas Aquinas

I completed my undergraduate work at the University of San Diego. It's a beautiful campus that overlooks Mission Bay, right around the corner from Old Town. While there, I had the opportunity to meet a number of extraordinary people.

One classmate, Mari Carmen Casta, was a superb tennis player. She was also a member of USD's tennis team. As a member of the team, Mari Carmen was often off playing somewhere in competition for the school instead of studying.

Since we were both psychology majors, we met each other in class. While chatting one day, we made an agreement that she would teach me how to play tennis if I would tutor her. We kept the deal and, as a result, we became good friends.

After graduation, Mari Carmen became a highly ranked professional. Because of our friendship, we stayed in touch, and a few years after our graduation, Mari Carmen decided to get married and invited me to her wedding.

At her reception, I sat beside her college tennis coach, USD's Scott McCarthy. I had recently opened my first martial arts school, and as a martial arts instructor, I was eager to find out if Scott had any advice about becoming a better coach.

After making some small talk, I asked him what ages he enjoyed coaching most. Scott explained that during the summer, he taught kids from about eight to fourteen and he enjoyed watching these children grow.

Since many of my students were children, I wanted to get Scott's insight about how to look for the kids that would excel. So, I asked him what types of kids succeeded and went on to do bigger and better things in tennis.

After giving the question some serious thought, Scott told me that he often saw kids that came to tennis camp with lots of natural ability. During games, their natural "talent" allowed them to beat nearly all of their opponents. They relished being good, but since they thought that it was their ability that made them good, they didn't practice much, if at all.

On the other hand, kids with not as much natural "talent" would get beaten by these talented kids. Instead of thinking they didn't have what it took, these not-so-talented kids practiced. As they practiced, they became better. After about six months or so, their skills were so improved they could beat those "talented" kids.

These young tennis players were using the growth mindset. Using the growth mindset, these not-so-talented kids went on to become high performers. On the other hand, the talented ones, the ones with the fixed mindset, would quit.

This is why mindset is so important. The mindset you bring into your life daily will make a huge difference in the type of outcomes you receive.

Later, we'll talk about how to adopt a growth mindset and put it to work for you.

For now, let's examine how your body affects your mind.

Chapter 14

What's Going on With Your Body?

"Relax your body, and the rest of you will lighten up."

—Haruki Murakami

I had a client, let's call him Al, who frantically called me one day. I asked him what was going on. He told me that his business was struggling and he needed to see me right away, so we set up an appointment.

When Al walked in, his shoulders were slumped, his face focused on the ground in front of him.

I asked him how he was feeling.

"Depressed", he answered.

Now before we go on, let's quickly discuss two types of depression. They are Depression with a big "D" and depression with a little "d."

Little "d" depression is when you feel sad. This is the feeling that you want to just lie around on the couch all day.

Depression with a little "d" is when things in your life aren't going quite as well as you'd like. You had a bad day at work, you had a fight with your spouse, you're stuck in traffic and you're late, so now you feel a little down. This is depression with a little "d."

By the way, this used to be known as having the blues. Over the years, drug manufacturers have used advertising to relabel this as depression. Despite what drug manufacturers would like to convince you to believe, drugs aren't very helpful for getting rid of the blues.

On the other hand, big "D" depression is when you can't get even out of bed. It's a disease.

This disease can aggravate many other mental health problems and can result in a multitude of physical problems as well. It causes your self-confidence to plummet and eventually will cause you to withdraw from life itself.

If you are depressed with a big "D," you need to call a mental health professional right away.

To get a better idea about how Al was feeling, I asked him, "Have you eaten today?"

He told me he had (which was a good indicator he wasn't "big D" depressed).

Then I asked. "What do you think is making you feel depressed?"

Al began to tell me a story about his business. He felt anxious about his business because after having a couple of very successful years, business wasn't coming through the door the way it had in the past. His revenue was down and he was worried that if this continued, he wouldn't be able to pay his bills.

His answer told me that, although Al was feeling down, he wasn't actually depressed. Instead, his worries were weighing him down. His worries felt so heavy that he was starting to feel his life was out of control.

Al's zombie mind was reacting to this "weight." The heaviness he felt told him that something was wrong. As a result, he felt worried and anxious, mentally and physically.

This is why his shoulders hunched and his eyes focused on the ground. The weight he was feeling was pushing him down.

The input his zombie mind was giving his body was putting him in a powerless state. It was this state, or his physiology, that was causing him to feel weighted down.

His body was telling his mind how he was feeling and his mind simply reinforced it. This mind-body loop was keeping him focused on the problem.

Here's what happens when you focus on the problem.

When you focus on the problem, your mind disconnects from finding solutions. When you can't see a solution, it can make it impossible for you to what's needed to move forward.

Your Zombie Mind in Action

As you probably picked up from Al's story, the way you hold your body affects the way your feel. Your state, how you control your physiology, is the final element of the convergence triad. Simply put, your state is your posture. It is your posture, the way you hold your body, that prepares you physically for success or failure.

How?

Simply put, your posture will give you confidence or strip it completely away from you.

Confident people are relaxed. Their state, how they hold their bodies, communicates how they feel about themselves to the rest of the world. Even more important is that it communicates how they feel about themselves to themselves.

Why is feeling confident so important?

It's because we view confident people as leaders, movers, and shakers.

They are people whom we like, listen to, and trust.

White Belts and the Zombie State of Mind

The reason I could easily tell what was going on with Al was his physical reaction to the pressure he was feeling was similar to what I observed in white belts as they began sparring the first time.

For those who aren't familiar, sparring is part of nearly all martial arts systems. It is simply learning how to use your fighting techniques in a safe or controlled environment.

The idea behind sparring is to get a student familiar with being attacked by another human being. This way they can learn an appropriate response, rather than reacting irrationally if they are actually attacked.

Most people react irrationally in a conflict.

Why do people react irrationally in conflicts?

It's because the zombie mind often mislabels the conflict as a real or actual threat. It then starts an automatic routine to keep you safe.

This threat doesn't need to be real or physical.

You don't need to have a mountain lion leaping at you with teeth bared.

The threat only needs to be perceived as an attack.

This can be when you have a slightly heated disagreement with a coworker about how to proceed with a project or with your significant other on when and how the house should be cleaned. What happens in these situations is your zombie mind reacts, rather than responds, to the situation.

Reacting vs. Responding

An easy way to think about the difference between reacting and responding is when you are sick and are given medicine to help you get over your illness. If you react to the medicine, this is bad. A reaction means your body is rejecting or fighting the medicine; it is sending your body out of control.

On the other hand, if you respond to the medicine, this means the medicine is doing what it's supposed to do. It is helping you get over your illness. The medicine is working with your body to help you get better.

Reacting when you are in a conflict isn't useful, but it's normal. That's because it's an automatic routine that has been programmed into your zombie mind for thousands of generations.

Over the last few hundred thousand years or so, our bodies and minds have been programmed from birth with what's known as the acute stress response. More commonly, this is called the fight, flight or freeze response.

This response either freezes you in place, or gets your body ready to fight or run away in a situation your zombie mind *perceives* as dangerous.

When you are threatened, or perceive you are being threatened, your zombie mind takes over and sends you into one of the three responses that has been programmed into you over thousands of generations. Your body automatically reacts this way every time your zombie mind believes you are in danger.

This was a positive thing when your ancestors were on the savannas. Their acute stress response kept them alive and part of the gene pool.

It's a major part of the reason you're here today.

The problem, as we'll see, is that it can still put you in this hyper-vigilant state when the only threatening thing that has happened was your toast being burned.

So you can better understand how this works, let's take a quick look at what happens inside your body to send you into this state.

As soon as you perceive danger, your hypothalamus, a pea-sized portion of your brain located at the top of your brain stem, automatically activates two systems: the sympathetic nervous system and the adrenal-cortical system.

The activation of your sympathetic nervous system sets off a type of complex Rube Goldberg operation, where your adrenal medulla sends a signal to your adrenal glands telling them to release epinephrine and norepinephrine, two highly potent hormones.

As the sympathetic nervous system sends these hormones into your bloodstream, your hypothalamus also releases cortico-trophin-releasing factor (CRF) into your pituitary gland, which in turn tells your adrenal-cortical system to release another thirty or so hormones into your bloodstream.

These drugs cause your heartbeat and respiration to speed up, your blood pressure to skyrocket, and your muscles to become tense and ready for battle. Your body is ready to take on the threat.

But there is a problem.

Even though these drugs have made your body ready to fight, flee, or freeze, you react instead of responding.

Why is this a problem?

Because your automatic reactions take you down a dark path that leaves you in the panic mode.

The Panic Mode

When white belts first learn to spar, most go into the panic mode.

Why?

It's because their acute stress response kicks in.

When sparring, the fight or flight response does exactly what it's supposed to do. It kicks up the heart rate and respiration and tenses the muscles, getting you ready for action.

While a certain level of anxiety gets a person ready for battle, too much stress causes a martial arts student to become so agitated that they start to breathe rapidly and shallowly. Sometimes so much so that they hyperventilate and need to sit down to breathe into a paper bag.

You already know the physiology behind why this happens, but why did the student lose control even though they knew they were safe?

The student loses control because their acute stress response shuts down the part of their brain that allows them to control their behaviors.

This part of the brain is called the forebrain, or prefrontal cortex.

The forebrain's job is to use the information your brain takes in from your eyes, ears, nose, mouth, and skin, and make sense of it. Using this information, it quickly decides what actions you should take.

In other words, one of your forebrain's main jobs is to regulate your behavior.

Here's the problem.

If your senses take in any cues that that you associate with a threat, real or not, it is immediately processed to trigger your acute stress response. What's amazing about this operation is that it happens instantaneously, even before you even consciously perceive the danger.

This is because it can save your life in a truly threatening situation.

For example, you're walking down the sidewalk and a car suddenly swerves in your direction. Your fight, freeze or flight response automatically helps you jump out of the way.

But there's also a problem.

Too much cortisol short-circuits the operation of your hippocampus, which is responsible for organizing your memories of past dangers and anxiety-provoking experiences. Now you only have tiny pieces of these memories to call on for your present threat.

This means that your prefrontal cortex doesn't have enough information to figure out whether this threat is real or not. Now, your amygdala, which is a part of the primitive brain that's also found in lizards, takes over control because its job is to keep you safe.

While this is great for a real threat, like the car swerving in your direction, what if the threat isn't real?

What if your lizard brain takes control during a sparring match or while giving an important presentation in front of your boss?

When your lizard brain hijacks your prefrontal cortex, it makes it difficult, if not impossible, to regulate what you say and do.

It sends you to into the panic mode.

The first thing that happens as your prefrontal cortex becomes inoperable is you freeze, at least momentarily.

This is an excellent response to keep you from a predator's preying eyes It's not so great when someone throws a roundhouse kick at your head or if your boss asks a question that you don't have an answer for.

Next, your fight or flight response kicks in, telling you to duck the roundhouse or your boss's question or to throw a front kick as fast as you can or give a smart, knee-jerk answer that implies that anybody should know the answer to that.

These types of responses just aren't productive.

In the panic mode, white belts and businesspeople become feebleminded as their prefrontal cortex becomes inoperable. Their lizard brain turns them into a zombie.

Here's another important fact.

If this happens often enough, it can cause permanent damage to your mind and body.

While your body's normal process to a perceived threat is to activate the acute stress response and then go back to a normal, more relaxed state, when you stay stressed for long periods of time, like Al was, your acute stress response stays activated and puts excess strain on your physiology.

This is why Al's shoulders were slumped, and his head was tilted toward the ground.

Since his zombie mind was in control, Al's prefrontal cortex was being so affected that he was unable to properly process the information he was taking in. So, he kept seeing problems when he should have been looking for solutions.

If you're in the panic mode, focused only on defending yourself, your forebrain can't look for solutions. You are being controlled by your lizard brain and your lizard brain is only thinking about survival.

This is why when you are stressed, you say and do things that you later regret. When your prefrontal cortex is taken out of the equation, you are less able to regulate what you say and do.

As a result, you lose control. Of course, this is a recipe for disaster for your personal and professional lives.

On top of that, being constantly stressed is bad for your short- and long-term health.

What's really scary is that studies have found that being in a constantly stressed state has been linked to maladies like heart disease, cancer, stroke, and diabetes.

That is just the start.

This is why it is essential to know how to control your state. It's the only way you can keep the zombie mind from hijacking your thinking and shortening your life.

A little later in this book, you'll learn how to use your state to keep your lizard brain from taking control.

First, lets take a look at outcome-based thinking.

Chapter 15

Outcome-Based Thinking

"Once there were 3 bricklayers. Each one of them was asked what they were doing.
The first man answered gruffly, 'I'm laying bricks.'
The second man replied, 'I'm putting up a wall.'
But the third man said enthusiastically and with pride, 'I'm building a cathedral.'"

—Author Unknown

Outcome-Based What?

The bricklayer story is an excellent illustration of outcome-based thinking, which is having a clear vision of what you want to accomplish.

There are three basic elements of outcome-based thinking.

The first is to take an honest look at and then acknowledging your present situation. This is often the most difficult step because it can be hard to acknowledge your faults.

For example, if you are overworked and anxious, admitting you're overworked and anxious can be hard. If you are 30 pounds overweight, admitting you are 30 pounds overweight isn't easy. If you are $100,000 in debt, admitting you're over your head can be humiliating.

But as anyone who has overcome any type of problem will tell you, the first step in overcoming the problem is acknowledging you have a problem.

The second element is to know, like the bricklayer, what is going to be the product of your efforts. Where do you want to end up? Do you want to be calmer and more productive? Do you want to fit in the same clothes as you did ten years ago? Do you want to reduce the anxiety caused by your debt?

What's your desired result or situation? This is known as a well-formed outcome. We'll examine this more deeply in just a moment.

The third and final element is to develop a plan, or path, that will take you from where you are now to where you want to be. Think of your plan as a map that guides you to where you want to be.

Maybe your plan is to learn how to prioritize your time better or to learn how to coach your direct reports so you can delegate more of your work. Maybe it's getting off your assets and getting into the gym or stopping the fast food habit and begin taking your lunch to work. Maybe it's taking a hard look at your spending and saving habits and choosing to do something different in the future.

While there are three steps to outcome-based thinking, there are two more steps that make it work. Let's call them steps four and five.

Step four is to put your plan into action because without action your plan is just wishful thinking. This is another sticking point for many people.

The final step is using the feedback you receive from your efforts to adjust your plan. This step is necessary because no plan will work exactly as you would like it to work.

We'll look at all of these steps again momentarily.

Outcome-based thinking is powerful because, no matter your goal, it will streamline your ability to achieve almost any life desire or goal. All you need to do is understand its basics and then put them into action.

Let Me Tell You What I Don't Want

Most people have no idea what they really want in life, but they more or less do know what they don't want. This results in them spending their lives moving away from the things they don't want to have in their lives.

For example, a person may take a job because they don't want to live in poverty. Now, if you're living in poverty, that's a good goal, because nobody likes or want to live under a bridge.

But once you've achieved your initial goal of not living on the street, you'll need another motivator. You'll need to find something which provides you with the income you need and more. You'll probably start thinking about a job that can provide you with a certain lifestyle and personal growth.

This is known as outcome-based thinking.

This is what we're going to look at next.

Chapter 16

Using Outcome-Based Thinking

"Begin with the end in mind."

—Stephen Covey

One day the students of a philosophy class came into their classroom to find a table with some items on it. As they sat down, instead of lecturing, the professor picked up a very large, empty mayonnaise jar and started filling it with rocks that were about two inches in diameter.

When he had filled the jar to the rim, he asked, "Is the jar full?"

The students looked carefully at the jar and then agreed that it was full.

Next, the professor picked up a box of pebbles. Slowly he poured them into the jar. When he finished pouring, he lightly shook the jar. As he did, the pebbles filled in the open areas between the rocks.

Looking at the students, the professor again asked, "Is the jar full?"

While some had to think for a while, they all finally agreed that yes, the jar was full.

Nodding, the professor picked up a box of sand. Holding a funnel in one hand, he poured the sand through the funnel into the jar. The sand filled the spaces between the rocks and pebbles.

Once more the professor asked, "Is the jar full?"

This time all the students responded in unison with a resounding "Yes."

"Excellent," said the professor, "I agree!"

The professor continued, "Imagine that this jar represents your life. The rocks are the important things, your family, your partner, your health, your children. These are the things in your life that, if everything else was lost and only they remained, your life would still be full."

"The pebbles are the other things that matter. These are things like your job, your house, your car. Important but replaceable. "

The sand is everything else. The small stuff."

This is what I want you to think about," the professor continued, "If you put the sand into the jar first there is no room for the pebbles or the rocks."

The professor waited for a few moments to let that thought sink in. Then he said, "The same goes for your life."

"If you spend all your time and energy on the small stuff, you will never have room for the things that are important to you. This is why it's critical that you pay attention to the things that are most important to your happiness. Play with your children. Take your partner out dancing. There will always be time to go to work, clean the house, give a dinner party and weed the garden."

Putting the Rocks in Your Life

You always want to start your day focused on what's most important. You, as the professor taught us, want to put the rocks in first.

How can you make sure you do this?

Stephen Covey, who wrote *The 7 Habits of Highly Effective People*,[3] called outcome-based thinking starting with the end in mind.

In the last chapter we talked about the goal of getting a job. Outcome-based thinking is when you are focusing not only on your goal, which is to have a job, but on what you want that job to provide you with.

Your outcome is the kind of life you desire. This is big picture thinking.

While short-term decisions can pull you out of poverty, thinking about and deciding on your long-term outcome motivates you to do the things you need to do in order to achieve what you want out of life.

This is the importance of the universe question that you first encountered in chapter 4. The reason the universe question is so powerful is because it gives you the ability to create a well-formed outcome.

It makes you focus on what's most important in your life. A well-formed outcome will help you to make your decisions based on long-term desires and goals.

Without a well-formed outcome, you'll constantly chase that new shiny object. You'll work hard, but not on the things that count.

This is where outcome-based thinking comes in.

By taking the time to figure out what you really want out of life, instead of running away from what you don't want, your mind will spend its time and energy focusing on achieving what you want.

A well-formed outcome will help you drop into the place where miraculous things happen, the zone.

---

[3] 2016, Mango.

Well-Formed Outcomes and the Zone

By focusing your mind on what's important, outcome-based thinking can help you access the flow state that we talked about earlier. You can't drop into the zone while working on mundane tasks, tasks that aren't moving you in the direction you want to go. You can't find flow state if you let yourself get mired in the sands of life.

You have to be doing something that you can give yourself to fully. Something that brings you joy and moves the needle forward for you personally, professionally, or spiritually.

This is where well-formed outcomes come in. They make it easier to immerse yourself in the work you are doing. This is how you accomplish more.

Let's examine the ingredients of outcome-based thinking to help you make sure you're putting the rocks in first.

Creating Well-Formed, Positive Outcomes

"Peak performers are highly motivated by a deep and personal sense of mission."

—Charles Garfield

There are four ingredients of outcome-based thinking. These four ingredients are:

1. **Stay positive.**
2. **Make the outcome about you.**
3. **Use the right context.**
4. **Do not harm.**

Let's take a look at each of these ingredients.

Stay Positive

While simple in concept, staying positive one can be the most difficult.

Why?

It's because, according to social psychologists, the human mind tends to focus on the negative. The theory is that since negative things can quickly cause bad results, we want to be aware of them as soon as possible.

While this might be a good strategy for staying aware of predators and competing humanoid tribes, it's not very useful when thinking about what you want your life to be like.

Except when keeping us safe, negatives just aren't good motivators.

To make an outcome motivating, it needs to be focused on what you want to happen instead of what you don't want to happen.

Let's say you are overweight. Ask yourself, what do I want? Some people might say, "I don't want to be overweight."

This simply isn't a positive outcome.

Here's something else to think about. When you say, "I don't want to be overweight," your brain doesn't hear the "don't." What your brain hears is, "I want to be overweight."

Having difficulty believing this?

Take a moment to do the following exercise.

Right this minute, whatever you do, don't think of a white horse. Just don't think of a white horse.

What are you thinking about right now?

A white horse, right?

I'm sure you got the point.

Instead of not doing, give yourself a positive, well-formed outcome.

How does a positive well-formed outcome work?

Ask yourself, "What do I want?"

You might say, "I want to look better."

"I want to feel healthier."

"I want to have more energy."

In this case, an over-reaching outcome might be, "I want to have a healthy weight that allows me to look and feel better and have all the energy I need to pursue my goals and dreams."

This is a well-formed positive outcome.

By asking the question, "What do I want?" you focus your mind on what you want, your desired outcome.

This is not possible with a negative outcome.

You can't engage in a process of "not doing," or "not wanting." You can only engage in the process of wanting or doing.

Stating your outcome in positive terms moves you toward the outcome you desire.

Make It About You

A well-formed outcome is not about your spouse, your child, your boss, or your mother-in-law, it's about you.

As anybody who has ever been in a relationship will tell you, a goal to have your significant other be nicer to you is an impossible-to-achieve outcome.

Why?

Your significant other has a mind of her or his own. You have zero ability to control their thoughts or actions.

On the other hand, creating an outcome of "Spending 30 to 60 minutes a day with my significant other and respectfully listening to him or her" is about you.

It is something YOU can do.

You are in in charge of your actions and behaviors. When you create goals that you are responsible for doing, you can take action to accomplishing them.

A well-formed outcome focuses your efforts on what you can control—YOU.

Stay in the Right Context

You need to state your outcome in a specific context rather than as a universal.

Why?

Because a specific outcome gives you more choices. A universal like "always" and "never" reduces them.

Let's take another look at the example of reducing your weight. Using a universal context just isn't productive.

For example, you wouldn't declare, "I always exercise at 6 AM every morning."

Why not?

This outcome reduces your choices. Your *only* choice every day is to work out at 6 AM.

But what if you needed to be at a work meeting at 6 AM or had to catch a plane flight?

Would you tell the people in your meeting that you couldn't make it because you had to exercise or start exercising on the plane?

Of course not!

A realistic choice would be to reschedule your workout to later in the day or after your plane flight. You could also choose to wake up earlier and then attend your meeting or catch the plane.

This is why a better outcome statement is, "I work out 5 days a week."

Your outcome is specific, working out 5 days a week, while giving you the flexibility you need when other things come up. And, as you know, other things are always going to come up.

This is why using specifics instead of universals increases the choices available to you.

Do No Harm

To be well formed, your outcome needs to be one that doesn't harm you or anyone else or your environment.

Having outcomes that only benefit you while hurting others is narcissistic at best, and downright sociopathic at worst.

I hope that this is self-evident. If not, I highly recommend that you see a mental health professional.

This Is Like Rome

"Rome was not built in one day"

—John Heywood

Okay, you know what you want, you have a positive outcome in mind, you've made it about you, you've put it in the right context and what you want will not hurt you or anyone else.

Now what?

The next step is to do put together your goals using an especially useful project management technique.

This technique has been used by anyone building anything for thousands of years.

Let's take an easy example, one many of us can relate to, at least at some level. Imagine you have been overeating and under- exercising for about a decade. As a result, you have become 50 pounds overweight.

Let's also say your weight is 225 pounds and you want to weigh 175 pounds.

While you could make your outcome "I weigh 175 pounds," this goal is not going to motivate you or anyone else. In fact, this goal is downright demotivating.

Why?

Before we look at the answer, let's look at another example, an example I'm very familiar with.

Let's say you wanted to write a book. You decide the book will be around 100 pages.

While you could make your outcome "I will write a 100-page book," I guarantee this goal will not merely demotivate you, it will completely demoralize you!

Why?

Because writing 100 pages is a very daunting task. Focusing on writing 100 pages will feel overwhelming.

While your big outcome can give you direction, to stay motivated, you need to be able to break that large goal into smaller pieces. The same way builders have done for thousands of years.

You need to focus on doing things one step at a time.

Chapter 17

Working Backwards

"The journey of 1000 miles starts with a single step

—Lau Tzu

As mentioned before, the late Stephen Covey said that to achieve anything we need to *"start with the end in mind."*
Think about it like this.

Builders have been constructing different types of structures for millennia. As any successful builder will tell you, before she begins, she decides what the building is going to look like.

Only after understanding what the final construction is going to look like will the builder make her plans.

Lifetime Outcomes

When creating outcomes, your big goals are known as *lifetime outcomes*. These are outcomes that align with your life's purpose and will take your lifetime to complete.

Professionally, this could be to create that $25 million company or become the CEO of a Fortune 500 company. Personally, this goal could be to be the best spouse or parent you could possibly be or working in a community group to improve an underdeveloped neighborhood.

Before we move on, take a few minutes and write two of your lifetime outcomes in your journal. One will be for your professional life the other for your personal life.

Long-Term Outcomes

Once you've decided on your lifetime outcomes, you can develop your *long-term outcomes*. Again, you want to create these for both your personal and professional life.

Long-term outcomes are goals that take a lot of time. A rule of thumb is it is a goal that takes at least one to three years to accomplish.

Long-term outcomes are buying a home, graduating from college, or starting your own business. Your long-term outcomes are what you use to reach your lifetime outcomes.

Take a minute and write down two long-term outcomes in your journal. One for your personal life and one for your professional life.

Milestones

Next, you create *medium-term milestones*.

In project management, milestones are simply checkpoints you've created to compare your progress with your plan. Milestones provide you with feedback. They keep you on track toward your desired end result.

Your medium-term milestones usually take anywhere from three months to a couple of years to complete.

A medium-term milestone could be the amount of money you need to save for the down payment on your home. It could be the funds needed to start your business. It could also be the number of classes you take each semester or quarter in school to graduate in a certain length of time.

All right, now it's time to write your milestones in your journal for the professional and personal goal you decided on.

Steppingstones

Now that you have your milestones, the last thing you need to do is break them into short-term tasks. These short-term tasks are steppingstones that move you along the path to your medium- and long-term goals. These tasks are the regular actions you take daily that move you toward your long-term outcome.

Having a goal to put a certain amount of each paycheck into a savings account for your home or business is motivating because it is something you can do. The goal of studying for a certain number of hours each week is motivating because it is a specific action step.

Breaking your long-term outcomes into short-term achievements helps you stay motivated. By setting small achievable tasks, you have the focus you need to drop into the zone because you are working on what you've defined as success.

Take a few minutes to write down the steppingstones you will need to take to reach your long-term outcomes or goals in your journal.

Well, now that you have all your basics, let's do some exercises.

PART II

Exercises

Introduction to Part II

"When you change the way you look at things, the things you look at change."

—Wayne Dyer

The following section contains techniques and processes that, when practiced, will help you take control of your thinking.

Why do you need to learn how to control your thinking? Because it's the only way you can learn to drop into the zone.

Let me tell you a story about Matt. When I met Matt, he was working as the nursery manager in a big-box store. After meeting Matt and having a little small talk, I asked him how he was doing. He told me he was "doing okay."

I replied, "That's great! What does 'doing okay' mean?"

Matt took a deep breath and said, "Well, I make pretty good money and my job's secure."

"That sounds great," I agreed. "What else?"

After taking another big breath, Matt didn't say anything for about a minute. Finally, he said, "I don't feel very happy."

I nodded, smiled, and said, "And?"

"Well, to tell you the truth, I wish I was running my own business."

"What kind of business?"

"Well, I used to have a landscaping business. I think I'd like to have a landscaping business again."

Matt went on to explain that he had owned a small landscaping business but had decided to give it up and go to college. After graduating from college, a friend introduced him to the big-box store manager. After talking about his background, the manager had hired him on the spot.

"But this is a good job," Matt said emphatically.

"So why are you here in my office?" I asked.

'Well, a friend of mine asked me what was happening with me one day. I told her I was feeling like I was being held back.

She said I sounded depressed, so I decided to go to a doctor."

I smiled and nodded.

Matt continued, "The doctor seemed to agree that I was depressed, so he prescribed Zoloft."

"How did that work?" I asked.

"It worked for a while, but after a while it just made me feel funny."

I raised my eyebrows, saying, "And?"

"It's hard to get out of bed and go to work. I feel stuck."

I could see the sadness in Matt's eyes. I knew exactly how he felt.

There have been many times in my life where I have felt stuck, unable to move forward in my personal and professional life.

I have had many negative experiences that, when I allowed myself to dwell on them, caused past fears to rise.

Then, when I tried to make plans about the future, I would worry about what might happen if I failed.

These feelings of stuck-ness made it easy for me to lose sight of what I wanted to accomplish and then fall into the trap of self-doubt.

What I've found is that when you fall into that trap, it can be very hard to dig yourself out.

Matt continued to see me every couple of weeks for about three months. During these sessions, he discovered that his real problem was he just didn't know what he needed to do to move forward in his life.

Have you ever felt like Matt?

Now, I don't necessarily mean you were diagnosed as being depressed, but did you felt stuck, as if some unseen force was holding you back?

Like I said, I have, and that's where my journey began.

I wanted to learn practices, like the ones you'll find in in this section, that could be put to use to help me get un-stuck.

That's one of the biggest things you're going to learn in this section.

How to un-stick yourself.

You see, what my research pointed out to me was there is a predictable pattern that leads to success or failure.

Let's take a look at that pattern.

The Amazing Human Animal

Over the past few millennia, we humans have accomplished some amazing things. Just in the last 50 years, we have traveled to the moon. We have eradicated smallpox, a disease that killed an estimated 300 million people in the 20th century alone. We carry computers (cellphones) around in our pockets that guide us (nearly) flawlessly to any destination and can communicate with people around the world.

What do all of these accomplishments have in common?

They all started with a thought in a human being's brain.

Like those accomplishments, everything you do starts with your thinking. It's your thinking that controls your actions.

When you repeat those actions enough times, they become habits. What you habitually do controls your focus.

You accomplish in life what you habitually focus on. As a result, your habitual focus becomes your destiny.

This is why it's so important that you learn to control your thinking. Because your thinking controls your destiny. It is the start and finish of everything.

This is how I helped Matt, by teaching him how to apply the techniques and processes you'll find in this section. Using these, he was able to take control of his thinking and drop into the zone.

As a result, Matt was able to do three times as much work with half the effort.

He worked on a business plan and opened his landscape business. He now employs a dozen or so like-minded employees.

This is the beauty of the skills you'll learn in this book.

These skills will help you to learn how to control your thoughts and drop into the zone.

In the zone, you can take the actions you need to get the right things done.

This is how you can accomplish the great things in life you want to achieve.

By taking action and getting things done.

That is what you want to do, right?

Excellent, then let's get started!

Chapter 18

This is Essential for Success

"He who has a why can endure any how."

—Friedrich Nietzsche

o you remember the two questions from Chapter 4? In case you've forgotten, they were:

"If all the forces in the universe suddenly came together for me, what would I want my life to be like?"

"If I were to win $10 million in the lottery, what would I do with my life?"

Have you been answering these two questions every morning since we've started training together?

If not, why not?

When you answer those questions in the morning, you're setting your day up for success. You have programmed your mind to look for solutions to find what you want, instead of being distracted by random thoughts and events.

So do the exercise!

Before starting the next group of exercises, let's talk about journaling.

Why journaling?

The only way to understand if anything is working is to keep track of your efforts. The easiest way to do this is by journaling.

What is Journaling?

Generally speaking, journaling is the process of recording the events of your day, your thoughts, ideas, inspiration, and anything else you wish to keep a record of.

In order to find out your best path to be able to drop into the zone, you're going to use a journal to keep track of the feedback you get from your results. This is the only way you can get better at using the skills and accomplish the things you want to get done.

You can go to https://tinyurl.com/Mindful-Mastery-Journal to get your FREE interactive journal especially designed for this book.

A Focus Problem

Most people don't take advantage of their results. In other words, they focus on their mistakes and how those mistakes might negatively affect them.

This way of thinking teaches you to avoid mistakes because mistakes are "bad." As a result, you avoid doing whatever you did again because you begin to believe you are "not good" at it.

As we already discussed earlier, this is a fixed mindset. This mindset will prevent you from learning anything from your results.

Having a fixed mindset is something you've learned. Over time, you've turned it into your habitual way of thinking. The problem with this habit is it will keep your thoughts stuck and hold you tightly in place.

You can't move forward in life with a fixed mindset.

Use Journaling to Change Your Mind

If you're not doing so already, you're going to start using journaling to help you change this mindset. Journaling will help you develop a new, positive habit.

Instead of focusing on your mistakes, what you did "wrong," you're going to teach yourself to use your journal by using your results to give you feedback. Then you're going to use this feedback to improve your performance.

This is how you develop a growth mindset and make it your habitual way of thinking.

The growth mindset presupposes that these so-called mistakes and problems are simply learning experiences. They are stepping-stones to the right answer. Instead of mistakes, you now define these experiences as feedback, something to help you correct your performance.

When you adopt this mindset, you can use your experiences to improve in all areas of your life. This is where journaling comes in.

You can use your journal like a scientist, recording and reflecting on what works for you and what doesn't. This allows you to make necessary adjustments to your efforts.

It will also help you keep track of your efforts, encouraging you, during tough times, to continue. When you run into a difficult problem, instead of saying, "this is too tough for me," you will be able to say, "I just haven't figured this out YET."

What should you use for your journal?

I'm old school and use pen and paper for my journal but don't let this keep you from using an electronic notepad, a blog, your phone or anything else that works for you.

You need to use a method that makes it easy, fun and interesting enough that you will be motivated to keep on using your journal every day for the rest of your life.

Your journal is a personal document designed to help you learn, grow, remember, improve, and achieve the goals you set for yourself. Your journaling doesn't have to be a masterpiece. It simply is a way for you to track your progress.

Here's what's key.

Make sure that while you're going through the exercises in this book, you write the results of your experiences in your journal. Do this every day.

What you're doing is teaching yourself to learn from your feedback.

So, if you haven't already written the answers to the two questions at the beginning of this chapter, do it now before moving on to the next exercises.

As the great philosopher Yogi Berra once said, *"If you don't know where you are going, you'll end up someplace else."*

That's where most people end up—someplace else.

On the other hand, peak performers know exactly where they are going. This is why they are more likely to end up there.

So, right now, take a minute and write down what you would imagine your life to be like in your journal.

Chapter 19

It's Time to Pay Attention!

"To pay attention, this is our endless and proper work."

—Mary Oliver

A mother walked her 7-year-old son to the bus stop one morning. They waited patiently until the bus came and the boy got on the bus. She waved as the bus pulled away and then went back home to finish getting ready for work.

About 15 minutes later, she was just about ready to leave when the doorbell rang. She opened the door and was amazed to see her son standing there.

Looking past her son, she saw the school bus with its door open and the bus driver interestedly watching.

Looking down again at her son she asked, "What are you doing back home? Did you forget something?"

"No," the boy answered, "I just decided I'm quitting school. It's too hard, it's too boring, and it's too long."

Fighting back a smile, the boy's mom took a deep breath and answered, "That's just how life is. Now get back on the bus."

As you continue to practice these exercises, you may feel a little like the boy in this story. Nevertheless, if you really want to get unstuck, you are going to have to practice your exercises every day. You have to get on the bus.

Who's in Charge Here?

> *"Life is an act—most of it, anyway. Get out there today and pretend you're in charge, for goodness' sake. Do you hear me? Lift up your head and pretend." A flicker of a smile passed over her face. "It's the secret to everything."*

> —**Kate Alcott,** *The Dressmaker*

Are You Really in Charge?

If you ask someone who is in charge of their thoughts, how will they respond?

They will tell you, "I am in charge of my thoughts."

But are they really?

For most people their thoughts are wandering about randomly, never staying in one place long enough to accomplish anything of real importance.

There's a good chance your thoughts might be wandering also.

Here are two questions I want you to answer right now.

First, are you in charge of your thoughts?

Second, do you think your thoughts on purpose?

While most people believe that they are thinking the thoughts they want to think, when we take a closer look, very little of what they are giving thought to is what anybody would call purposeful thinking.

In fact, most people's thinking is not purposeful at all.

Don't believe me?

Here's a simple way to check.

For the next minute, the only thing I want you to do is think about one thing: your breathing.

Here's how you're going to do it.

For a mere sixty seconds you are going to keep track of your thoughts.

The first thing you're going to do is grab a piece of paper and a pen or pencil. Put it somewhere where you can use them to make a mark easily.

What you're going to do is put a mark on the paper every time a thought besides thinking about your breaths comes into your mind.

The second thing you'll do is set a timer on your phone for sixty seconds.

The third thing is to find a comfortable place to sit. You can sit in a chair, on your sofa, on the floor. Anyplace where you can sit comfortably with your back straight for 60 seconds.

Fourth, hit "start" on your alarm and close your eyes.

Try to think only about your breathing for the next 60 seconds. Every time a thought besides breathing comes into your mind, make a mark on your paper.

Finally, in your journal write down your results. How many marks did you make on that piece of paper?

I'm hallucinating (I hallucinate because I'm not there and I am writing this in your past) that, if you were honest with yourself, you have quite a few marks on that piece of paper.

Here's what you need to know: this is completely normal.

Here's something else you need to know.

You can use the processes and techniques you'll find in this book to take better control of your wandering mind.

All it takes is some time and effort.

Like I tell my clients, if you're willing to do some work, then I'm willing to help you.

If this is a deal, read on.

If not, close this book and give it to someone else who is willing to do the work because. Like the little boy, you have to get on the bus to get results.

If you're determined to continue then let's take a look at why paying attention is so important and how you can become better at doing it.

Chapter 20

Keeping Track of Your Zombie Beliefs

"You are only as limited as your beliefs."

—Jennifer Ho

One of the limiting beliefs I had growing up and well into my twenties was that I wasn't very good with mechanical things. I felt my manual dexterity just wasn't very good at all. While it took me a long time to recognize it, I adopted this belief because of the interactions I had with my father as a very young boy.

My father grew up on a farm in Wisconsin. During the Great Depression, he went to work for President Franklin Delano Roosevelt's Conservation Corps, working on building and repairing U.S. Park facilities.

During World War II, he was an airplane mechanic, working for the Air Task Force of the United States Army in China. After the war, he opened his own auto repair and body and fender shop in Los Angeles.

As you probably figured out from his job descriptions, my dad was an excellent mechanic and excellent with his hands. He could do mechanical things quickly and easily.

When I was four or five years old, I wanted to be like my dad. When he was working on the car, I wanted to help.

Inevitably, since I was so young, I would drop the screw or wrench a few times, well maybe more than a few times. Losing patience, my dad would grab the wrench and say something like, "Ahh! Let me do that!"

After experiencing this quite a few times, I started to think of myself as not being good at repairing things with my hands. As a result, I went through my teenage years believing I didn't have good mechanical manual dexterity.

Fast-forward fifteen years. The U.S. Navy spent thousands of dollars training me as an electronics technician.

One of the things I had to learn to do as an E.T. was work with my hands in very small spaces. For example, putting nuts and small screws into circuit boards or attaching electronics parts to the frames of equipment I worked on.

One day, as I was putting a nut on a screw in the back of a chassis of a piece of crypto equipment, I suddenly realized that I was pretty dexterous. I was actually good at working with my hands!

What was even more interesting is that as soon as that thought entered my brain, my zombie mind must have gone back to my childhood, because I immediately dropped the nut!

Then, for the next five minutes, I had to dig around in the back to fish it out.

Thanks, zombie mind!

Right now, I'm presuming that you have some beliefs stored in your zombie mind that are just not very helpful. This might be a belief like, "I'm not good with money," "I'll always be overweight," or I could never be athletic."

Maybe this passage has reminded you of a few of your limiting beliefs. If it did, write them down, in your journal.

(You can go to https://tinyurl.com/Mindful-Mastery-Journal to get your FREE interactive journal especially designed for this book.)

Today, every time you have a thought like that, write it down. If you don't carry your journal with you, write them in a notepad or put them in the notepad on your phone.

A little later in this book, we'll look at how to use this process to help you drop the doubt so you can drop into the zone.

But for right now, just make sure you jot down your limiting beliefs.

Here's why.

Often your zombie storehouse only gives you glimpses of your limiting beliefs. The only way you can turn a limiting belief around is to know it's there.

Once you have the ability to recognize them, you will be able to label them for what they are: a figment of your zombie mind.

This is it for this exercise.

Now let's add some years to your life.

Chapter 21

This Will Add Life to Your Years

"Breathe. Let go. And remind yourself that this very moment is the only one you know you have for sure."

—Oprah Winfrey

While bacteria, ants, termites, cockroaches and a few other lifeforms beat us out, we humans are one of the most adaptable species on the planet. We can live in the coldest mountain climates as well as in the harshest, hottest deserts. We can fly high above the earth in spacecraft and dive far below the sea's surface in submarines.

These fantastic abilities can make us pretty darn sure of ourselves. This is unless we lose access to one of three simple things.

These are food, water and air.

Without any of these three, we quickly become food for the cockroaches.

On average, you can live three weeks without food. You can live about three days without water. But when it comes to breathing, you can only last about three minutes (more or less) without air, or more accurately, the oxygen in the air.

In modern society, we have access to plenty of food and water. Since the time humankind started walking around on the planet, there has been plenty of air for us to breathe. Today, you can even buy "fresh air" from companies around the world. However, even though air is usually readily available, many people aren't really getting enough air.

Why?

It's because of the way we breathe.

Slow Suffocation

There are four types of breathing: eupnea, hyperpnoea, diaphragmatic, and costal breathing. Each type requires slightly different processes.

Let's take a quick look at the four types of breathing.

1. **Eupnea** is normal quiet breathing. It could also be called "normal" breathing. This type of breathing requires the contraction of the diaphragm and external intercostal muscles.

2. **Diaphragmatic** breathing involves deeper breathing than eupnea breathing. It requires the contraction of the diaphragm and is also called deep or belly breathing.

3. **Hyperpnoea** is forced breathing. This is when you're breathing in more air but not necessarily breathing faster. It requires muscle contractions during both inspiration and expiration such as contraction of the diaphragm, intercostal muscles, and accessory muscles. This type of breathing can happen during exercise or because of a medical condition that makes it harder for your body to get oxygen, like heart failure.

4. **Costal** breathing is a mode of breathing that requires contraction of the intercostal muscles. As the intercostal muscles relax, air passively leaves the lungs. This type of breathing is also known as shallow breathing because the lower lungs are not getting oxygen.

While there are four types of breathing, we're only going to focus on two. The first is diaphragmatic and the other is costal.

Diaphragmic breathing fills your body and mind with large quantities of oxygen. Costal breathing can and often will leave you breathless and clueless.

Babies and small children naturally fully engage their diaphragm to take deep, refreshing breaths. The same goes for everyone who is sleeping or deeply relaxed.

This is why this type of breathing, where air fills the whole lung, is sometimes called natural breathing.

The problem is, as we get older, we get out of the natural breathing habit. As a result, we stop using our full lung capacity.

Everything from the stresses of everyday life, to the practice of "sucking in" the stomach for the appearance of a trimmer waistline, gradually shifts our breathing to the shallower, less satisfying chest or costal breathing.

When you breathe like this, you are only breathing into the upper portion of your lungs. This leaves fifty percent of your lungs uninflated and without oxygen. This leaves you without the fuel needed to operate at even a normal level.

Learning to Breathe Again

I've taught martial arts to thousands of students. What I found is many had forgotten how to breathe deeply. This prevents them from getting enough oxygen. As a result, these students needed to learn how to breathe again.

I did this using a mindfulness technique known as belly breathing.

This exercise helped them re-develop the habit of breathing diaphragmatically. It can help you breathe better too.

Belly breathing is a great way to untangle yourself from difficult emotions and mental preoccupations. Difficult emotions are usually events from the past. Mental preoccupations have more to do with worrying about the future.

As you learn to focus on your breath you can leave the past behind. You also gain a better understanding that the future can only be achieved by being fully present. This will allow you to clear away obstructions while gaining a clearer vision of what you want.

By concentrating on your breath, you heighten your awareness of what's going on in your body, right now. This helps you to find stressful places in your body and let them relax.

This practice teaches you how to spend more of your time in the present.

Now, instead of spending time in the past, or dreaming about the future, you are present, in the now, the only place you can get things done.

Here's why.

For most people, danger is something they imagine, or what I would say, "hallucinate," about in the future. You might hallucinate about what would happen if you lost your job or if your significant other left you.

Your regrets live only in the past. When you feel regret, take a step back. You will probably find that although you prefer that those events had gone differently, you gained wisdom by going through them.

This is the wisdom you are using today in your life.

By learning to live more in the present, you'll find that your habitual repetitive anxious thinking about the past and future starts to fade. Now you have more time and energy to use your brain for the things it was made for: problem solving, creativity, appreciating music, etc.

It will also eliminate nearly all of your problems.

Living in the present simply means paying attention to what you're doing right now. Observing what your five senses are telling you. This is what the upcoming exercise is about.

This exercise was originally printed in my book *Secrets of the Black Belt Mindset, Turning Simple Habits into Extraordinary Success.*

Harnessing the Amazing Power of Your Breath

The following are the steps to master belly breathing. Use them to help you focus your mind on the present.

1. Put one hand lightly on your stomach and your other hand lightly on your chest.

2. Take a gentle breath in through your nose, drawing the air deeply into your lower lungs.

3. Without trying, let your belly expand. Don't put any effort into its expansion. Just let your lungs fill with air. The air will also fill the upper portion of your lungs. Only the hand on your belly should move outward, not the hand on your chest.

4. Exhale slowly through your nose. Feel your stomach contract as you breathe out. Make sure you push all the air out of your lungs. It should take slightly longer for you to exhale than to inhale.

5. Continue to take in and let out your breaths slowly. Pay attention to the expansion and contraction of your belly. At a minimum you should take in five to seven breaths. To make this an even more valuable experience, practice for a minimum of three to five minutes.

6. Practice, practice, practice!

Practice belly breathing at home, at work, in the car, when you go shopping. And don't worry about your hand positions. These are only to help you in the beginning.

Practice everywhere you go. In no time at all you'll find yourself using diaphragmatic breathing automatically.

The wonderful thing about this technique is it helps to quickly calm your body and mind, anytime and anywhere. It also brings your mind into the here and now, the only place you can accomplish anything.

Before you go to bed tonight, practice this exercise and write down your experience in your journal.

(You can go to https://tinyurl.com/Mindful-Mastery-Journal to get your FREE interactive journal especially designed for this book.)

That's all there is to this exercise!

Now, let's move on.

Chapter 22

You'll Never Achieve Anything Without This One Thing

"If you don't know where you're going, anywhere you end up will do."

I don't know who this quote is from, but I did hear Zig Ziglar tell a story about a traveler who goes to buy a plane ticket at an airport.

The traveler goes up to the counter agent and says, "Give me a ticket."

The agent looks up and asks, "Where would you like to go?"

The traveler replies, "That doesn't matter, just give me a ticket."

Looking concerned, the agent pleasantly replies, "I'm sorry, you have to have a destination for me to sell you a ticket."

Again, the traveler says, "No, a ticket to anywhere will do. Just give me a ticket."

Before we go any further, let me ask you a question. If you were that counter agent, what would you do?

I'm hallucinating that, unless that person started laughing at you, saying "I got you, didn't I?" you'd probably seriously think about calling security. In fact, you might even call security as soon as he walked away.

Why?

Because there must be something off if a person wants to buy an airline ticket without a destination, right?

Here's the question you need to ask yourself: "What do I want out of this book?"

Maybe you're thinking, "That's a strange question. Shouldn't you be telling me what I should get out of this book?"

Well, the answer is no. I have no idea what you should get out of this book.

The purpose of this book is to help you take control of your thinking. This can help you take charge of your life.

Here's the point. To take charge of your life, you, like the airport passenger, have to first figure out where you're going.

So, what is it that you intend to achieve?

Here's the first thing I want you to do.

Write down what you intend to get out of this book.

For example: "My intention for reading and doing the exercises in this book is to improve my focus and concentration."

Second, write down how you'll measure it.

Here you could write, "The way I will know I have accomplished this is I can keep my mind focused for (3, 5, 15 seconds, minutes, hours, days) at a time so I can drop into the zone."

Finally, write down what you're willing to give for what you want.

"To achieve this, I will practice my exercises for 15 minutes every morning and every evening."

What you're trying to do here is establish a habit.

But first, do the exercise.

Let's review the steps:

1. What do you intend to achieve?

2. How will you measure it?

3. What are you willing to do to get it?

Do this exercise NOW!

(You can go to https://tinyurl.com/Mindful-Mastery-Journal to get your FREE interactive journal especially designed for this book.)

Don't worry about how long this takes or if you get it perfectly correct. The goal here is to start thinking about setting your intention.

All right, this is it for this exercise!

Right now, stand up and say, "Awesome job, (your name here)!"

Now, let's move on to controlling your zombie response.

Chapter 23

Controlling Your Zombie Response

"We are what we repeatedly do. Excellence, then, is not an act, but a habit."

—Aristotle

Back in Chapter 7 we took a look at your zombie response. As you learned, your zombie response is the reason behind how you cross your arms, brush your teeth, or drive.

It's also the reason behind other, more insidious habits like reaching for that candy bar or bag of potato chips or yelling at your spouse or coworker when you're stressed. It's why you go home and flop on the couch, drinking your favorite hard or soft drink and munching on snacks instead of stopping at the gym to exercise.

Your zombie response is behind nearly everything you do.

This is because your zombie response is what forms your habits.

In his book *The Power of Habit*,[4] Charles Duhigg writes about three steps that create behavior. He calls these three steps, cue, routine and reward, the "Habit Loop."

The writer and speaker James Clear renamed these three steps the 3 Rs: Reminder, Routine, and Reward. We're going to use this because it's easier to remember three R's.

How the Habit Loop Works

First, you get a **reminder**, also known as a trigger.

The reminder is what brings your attention to something you do on a regular basis or habitually. This trigger could be the ding on your phone telling you that you just received an update on Facebook, hearing a particular song or having tortilla chips delivered to your table at a Mexican Food restaurant, which is a huge trigger for me.

Next, your reminder, or trigger, causes you to go into your automatic **routine**.

In the case of the phone ding, you grab your phone to see which of your 900 closest friends just posted what they are eating for lunch. Another reminder is the song that makes you to go into the routine of smiling, or crying.

Me, my routine is I see the chips and then start stuffing big handfuls of them into my mouth.

Now, here comes your **reward**.

Studies have found that in many cases, your reward is a release of brain chemicals like dopamine and other neurotransmitters. These chemicals make you feel relaxed and happy and help you to feel good.

Now that you've received your reward, you're feeling really good, at least for the moment. That is, until you realize you haven't

---

[4] 2014, Random House.

gotten your work done or you've just moved a little further away from your healthy weight goal.

Now you start to feel guilty, powerless, and out of control. This can even make you feel sad and depressed.

Why did you do this, even though you knew it wasn't good for you? It's because your zombie mind took over again.

Does this mean that you are locked into those behaviors forever?

No, not at all. You can take back control of your zombie mind.

Recognizing the Zombie Response (Back to Awareness)

Here's the good news. Unlike the viruses in the movies that take over your mind and make you unable to think for yourself, turning you into a zombie, habits are learned.

The better news is if you learned it, you can unlearn it.

But to unlearn it, you must notice it.

You need to become aware that your habit exists; just like when you were learning to tie your shoes or put on your clothes, you're going to have to pay attention to what you are doing.

This is because the recognition of your triggers and habits is the first step to zombie recovery. Before you can unlearn anything, you need to become aware of what you're doing.

You need to pay attention.

What you're going to do for this exercise is begin to pay attention to your triggers.

For example:

When you reach for the chips, cookies or beer.

When you feel angry or upset at a coworker or your significant other.

When you reach for your phone when you're supposed to be working.

You can add any trigger you want.

For now, all you're going to do is keep track of your zombie responses, just like your zombie beliefs.

Again, do this in the moment, when the trigger happens. Put it in your notepad or your phone's notepad.

Don't let these thoughts slip away without capturing them. This is important for zombie recovery.

At the end of the day, transfer these thoughts into your journal.

(You can go to https://tinyurl.com/Mindful-Mastery-Journal to get your FREE interactive journal especially designed for this book.)

Now let's move on to figuring out how to determine what direction you need to head to.

Chapter 24

Finding Your True North

"As a well-spent day brings happy sleep, so a life well spent brings happy death."

—Leonardo da Vinci

rue, or geodetic, north is the direction along the earth's surface towards the geographic North Pole. Polaris, the current North Star, sits almost motionless in the sky above the pole.

Seafaring people have used true north to navigate for millennia. You can use true north to navigate to exact points on the earth. It helps you get to where you want to go.

What Counts?

To get to where you want to go in life, you need to know where YOUR true north is. If you don't, your zombie mind will keep pulling you off track and you will find yourself going in a different direction from your conscious goals.

So how do you find true north?

You have to figure out what counts the most, for you.

The universe question was to get you to think about life with no constraints. This helps you think about how you start with the end in mind.

You're going to use that information to help you with this exercise.

But, before we go through this exercise, take a moment to think about the following example.

Let's say you've decided that, to live your preferred lifestyle, you need to create a business that has gross sales in excess of 25 million dollars a year and earns you a million dollars take-home a year.

To become intrinsically motivated to accomplish this goal, you simply need to understand one thing: why you want to build the business.

Before I go on, as a business coach, I understand that you are going to have to come up with a strategy for your business. You're going to have to put together a plan to put your strategy into action. You're going to have to take action and you're going to have to monitor your results.

All of this is a given.

But for you to create a successful business, the one that will get you up in the morning, that will keep you working the long hours needed for its creation and sustainability, and enjoy the process, at least most of the time, you need to have a big why; you have to figure out your source.

The first thing you need to recognize is that, even if you are starting from deep poverty, your source simply isn't because you want to be rich. While becoming wealthy can be a rather enjoyable by-product of building your company and having your $1 million gross income, it, by itself, won't drive you to get out of bed in the morning.

For nearly all people, the goal of having a lot of money won't be the type of goal that builds passion into pursuing the process of building a business.

This is because for goals like this, your biology will work against you.

You develop outcomes, goals, or things that you want in your mammalian brain or your neocortex. It's called the mammalian brain because it is only present in mammals, not in birds or reptiles.

Your neocortex is responsible for reason, logic, and language. It gives you the ability to solve math problems and write e-mails. It's often called the conscious mind.

Your limbic brain, which is also present in birds and reptiles, is your feeling brain. It's responsible for your behavior.

Your limbic brain helps you make decisions. It has no capacity for language, so it doesn't communicate with words, but rather with feelings.

This is why you get a "feeling" about some things that happen. These feelings result from your limbic brain's evaluation of the input you're receiving from your senses and then trying to communicate it in a way that will make sense to you.

This brain is often referred to as the subconscious or unconscious mind. It's responsible for all your other-than-conscious processes, and, yes, for all your zombie behaviors as well.

Unless money is your real motivator, which, again, for nearly everyone this just isn't true, your conscious and other-than- conscious processes won't align.

Your conscious mind will be pulling you in one direction and your other-than-conscious processes in another. Because your mind is being pulled in two directions, you can't stay focused on your outcome.

Your lizard brain will win the battle for control of your behavior every time.

While I don't want to go too in-depth about how this works, I do want to give you a quick overview of why this happens. (You can find detailed information in my book *Secrets of the Black Belt Mindset*.)

Your brain takes in raw information every day through your nervous system. This raw information is known as sensations. This is what you see, hear, touch, smell, and taste. Your nervous system sends those sensations to your brain, which makes sense of it through a process called coding.

Your zombie mind takes in this information and examines it, comparing it to the information you've stored there. If the information it receives is in alignment with what it believes to be true, it will allow it to pass through unabated.

But if the information is not in alignment with the information stored there, then it will do everything in its power to correct your behavior so it can feel good about what you're doing with the information.

So, if your conscious outcome is to create a $25-million-a-year business so you can be rich and famous but your *highest value* is your personal freedom because of your past experiences, your conscious and other-than-conscious processes are going to be out of alignment.

This will result in a tug-of-war that only your lizard brain can win.

The good news is that there are ways to get your feeling and thinking brain configured to work together for peak performance. You can align your brains by aligning your values with your goals.

Understanding your values gives you your true north and this exercise is going to help you do just that.

Uncovering What You Really Value

To align with your lizard brain, the first thing you need to figure out are your values.

For this exercise, think of values as your priorities. Values are the things that matter most to you in your life.

Once you know your values, you can use them to guide you and help you prioritize events and people. This prioritization allows you to invest your time in a way that will help you get three times as much done with half the effort.

The Importance of Involving Your Zombie Mind in Your Choices

If you do this exercise quickly, picking whatever feels right to you, your zombie mind will be highly involved in your choices.

Given time to think, you may have an internal conversation that sounds something like, "I know I like play, but I don't think that's a very responsible choice so I'll choose work instead."

While it might make for a more responsible choice, it's not being honest or true to yourself. You won't be able to get your feeling and thinking brain configured to work together for your greatest good.

Here's an example.

When I first went through this exercise many years ago, I chose wealth as one of my core values. At that time, wealth, to me, was measured in dollars.

The problem with that choice for me is that I am not actually motivated by dollars; I am primarily motivated by personal growth and helping others. So, I would set goals to make a certain amount of money but wouldn't reach those goals because I was focused on the wrong thing.

When I changed my focus to be more in alignment with personal growth and helping others through teaching, my zombie mind went into overdrive trying to help me achieve the outcomes that I set for myself. I began researching and writing at a rate I had never reached in the past.

A side effect of these new, convergent goals was they also made me wealthier in the long term.

Directions:

1. Go through the following list and choose the top five values you feel are most important to you. If other values resonate with you that are not on this list, then, use them.

2. Do this quickly, picking whatever feels right to you and write them in journal.

3. Rank each item you picked from 1 (the most important) to 5 (the least important).

4. Decide which of the three basic psychological needs (Chapter 5)—relatedness (r), competence (c) or autonomy (a)—you fulfill by this value.

Write a short paragraph that explains why this value is important to you.

Do this exercise NOW!

Wealth	Challenge	Making a Difference	Fame	Play
Balance	Knowledge	Abundance	Family	Health
Learning	Work	Professionalism	Faith	Helping Others
Calmness	Excellence	Financial Independence	Fitness	Money
Teamwork	Prosperity	Open Mindedness	Freedom	Gratitude
Education	Midfulness	Personal Growth	Adventure	Public Service
Community	Relationships	Accomplishment	Sexuality	Discovery
Persistence	Sacredness	Self-Discipline	Spirituality	Imagination

(You can go to https://tinyurl.com/Mindful-Mastery-Journal to get your FREE interactive journal especially designed for this book.)

If you have done this exercise, you have found your North Stars!

Now that you have your North Stars, you can begin to navigate through your universe.

We'll come back to this a little later.

Right now, let's take a look at your beliefs.

Chapter 25

I Believe!

"If you always put limits on everything you do, physical or anything else, it will spread into your work and into your life. There are no limits. There are only plateaus, and you must not stay there, you must go beyond them."

—Bruce Lee

How would you live your life if you knew you could not fail?

Note: Although this chapter is in the exercise portion of the book, you'll find a lot of theory here. The reason for putting the theory you find here is to help you better put the exercises to use.

Your Guide

Your beliefs guide your actions.

You'll take action **IF** you believe your action will give you the results you want.

This is why people will develop and follow a certain business model. They believe that by taking the actions described in the model they have a greater chance of success.

This is also why some people will go on a specific diet in order to help them move closer to their ideal weight. They believe this diet will help them finally lose weight.

People take action **IF** they believe that the action they take will help them get to the outcomes they desire.

Beliefs make things simple. Beliefs act as shortcuts that let you know whether the action you're taking will get the results you're seeking.

They are generalizations about how the world works, based on your experiences, and give you a sense of certainty.

For example, what do you do when you want lights to go on in your house at night?

Unless you have automated lights or the Clapper, you'll flip the light switch on the wall.

So why do you flip the light switch?

Because your experience has given you a belief or a sense of certainty that when you flip the light switch, light will magically appear.

While you may not know the theory behind how electricity makes your lights work, you still are certain that the lights will appear when you flip the light switch.

You are *certain* that this result will happen every time you flip the switch, unless there is a problem with the lightbulb, the power or the light switch.

Let's say that by some extremely unlikely chance of fate, a Sentinelese islander, who is a person from arguably the most remote tribe on earth, suddenly appears at your house.

What will he do as the sun goes down and darkness begins to set in?

How will the Sentinelese islander bring light into the room?

A likely solution is that he will look for something to use as a torch and then, after finding what he needs, use two sticks and friction to start a fire. Using the fire they started, he would light the torch and bring light into the room.

Now, if the fire doesn't burn the house down, he can bring light into every room he walks into. While there could be many other ways the islander could start the fire, one thing is certain: he will never go over to the switch on the wall to light the room because it's not in his realm of experience.

Why?

It's because his experience has created a shortcut or generalization that says with certainty, "Light comes from fire. In order to light this area, I need to have fire. Let me find something I can use to start a fire and carry it with me."

Now you enter the room and, for the sake of this example, let's say you and the Sentinelese islander can speak the same language and the Sentinelese islander trusts you.

First, you ask for the torch and take it out of the house to keep the smoke from doing any more damage to your walls and ceilings.

Then you would patiently explain that the light switch brings light into the room.

Next, you demonstrate how to flip the wall switch and the lights would magically appear.

While at first the islander will probably think you are a witch doctor with some type of magical powers, since he trusts you, he'll try flipping the switch. When the light comes on, he'll understand he can take the same actions you do to fill the room with light.

As you go from room to room, showing him the light switch in every room, you allow them to try each one himself. As he does this, he will become more and more certain that he too can fill the room with light by flipping the switch.

Within a short time, the Sentinelese islander will know with certainty that the wall switch brings light into any room.

Question: Was the light always available?

Answer: Yes, of course the light was always available.

Question: Why didn't Sentinelese islander understand that? It was because his beliefs limited his ability to locate a light source. His beliefs controlled his search.

In the same manner, just like the islander, your generalizations limit how you experience your world.

In order for you to experience the world differently, you need to widen your search and expand your beliefs.

I'm Not Good Enough

By now, you'll probably agree that our beliefs can limit how we see the world. I'd like to share a personal example.

Many years ago, as I was sitting on a hardwood floor getting ready to take my first-degree black belt test, thoughts started going through my head. These were thoughts like, "What am I doing here? I'm not good enough to be a black belt! Maybe I should just stand up and leave."

These types of thoughts kept creeping through my mind as I sat there wondering if anyone had ever bolted from their black belt test before.

While I did feel like fleeing, I stayed and, because I passed the exam, I was awarded my first-degree black belt. But even this didn't change the thoughts I had about my abilities.

Even though the test had been quite difficult and I had performed all the requirements, I retained doubts. In my mind, I didn't have the skill level of the other black belts that had tested with me.

Fast forward six months or so.

A fellow black belt had been bringing a video camera to some classes and had taped many of our training sessions. One day, he brought a video tape (yes, it was a long time ago) of those classes to my house. Sitting down, I watched the video, mesmerized by how well one of the black belts in the background was performing his kicks, punches, and forms.

It was old technology and the picture was grainy. I tried to make out the black belt's face, but he was way in the back, hidden from view most of the time.

As I sat there thinking to myself, "Who could that guy be?" the camera zoomed in and, to my amazement, that black belt was me! I was that high-performing black belt in the background!

I asked my friend to lend me the video and I watched it at least a dozen more times. Each time I watched, I paid close attention to how my punches and kicks as well as my sparring compared to my classmates.

What I found amazed me. I was as good as any of them!

Watching that video changed how I saw my world.

My experience was the same as the Sentinelese islander exposed to a light switch for the first time.

Having the video's perspective allowed me to see myself differently. It gave me certainty about my skill level, which changed my level of belief in my abilities.

This shift in perspective gave me the confidence I needed to become a martial arts teacher and, eventually, a master martial arts practitioner.

That video showed me how to flip the switch in my life.

It led me think, "I believe in me!"

Chapter 26

The Myth of Talent

"Everyone thinks of changing the world, but no one thinks of changing himself."

—Leo Tolstoy

Successful people from every field are often seen as people who were born with exceptional ability or maybe just plain lucky.

Nothing could be further from the truth.

Roy Halladay had 12 seasons with the Toronto Blue Jays and four with the Philadelphia Phillies. Over his career in the big leagues he earned two Cy Young Awards.

What's fascinating about Roy was, after a promising start, he collapsed in his third season. His earned run average (ERA) rose to 10.64 and he was sent down to Class A baseball.

His wife, Brandy, bought him a book, *The Mental ABC's of Pitching*.[5] He devoured it and began handing out copies to his teammates. He devoted himself to the mental aspects of the game.

---

[5] Dorfman, H.A. (2017). Lyons Press.

He also devoted himself to physical fitness. He routinely put in 90-minute workouts before any of his teammates even made it to the clubhouse. His former pitching coach told Sports Illustrated that when other pitchers tried to do one of his workouts, they would nearly always quit halfway through.

Roy made the Hall of Fame not because of his talent, but because of his hard work, not because he was special.

Do You Have a Fixed Mindset?

Growing up, I had the typical North American mindset that we were either good at something or we weren't. Most of lower-middle class American boys, like me, believed that either we had a talent or we didn't.

It was that simple.

By the way, this is where the stereotype that Asians, particularly males, are good at math comes from. Some people believe that the Asian students have a special math gene that helps them do well in math.

As a boy, I knew I was okay at sports but I didn't think that I was as good as many of my peers. For example, I would play basketball with friends and would be adequate, but it seemed as though there were at least five or six other boys that were much better.

At the time, I thought that they must have had more talent than me for basketball. They were special.

Later, while in the U.S. Navy, I started to play basketball regularly. As I played more, I got better, enough to be invited to play in a lot of pickup games.

Even though I had improved, I can still remember thinking other players were more talented and, as a result, I would lose badly.

After one of these losses, my friends would ask, "Were you having an off day?" or questions of that nature.

Because I didn't think I was as good as the "talented players," I just thought they were joking. I knew in my mind I just didn't compare with their playing ability.

I just wasn't that special.

This is the attitude I brought with me into the martial arts. I believed that people with special talents always do better than people like me.

This is the textbook definition of a fixed mindset.

So what made me change my mind?

Practicing martial arts and studying Neuro-Linguistic Programming (NLP).

As you may already know, NLP is the study of how you can use the sensations you receive from your body, such as your ears, nose, mouth and fingers, to reprogram your mind for success. We'll talk about this a little bit more later.

Practicing martial arts and studying NLP taught me that I could improve, both mentally and physically, as long as I put in the effort.

Chapter 27

Do You Think You're Special?

"The moment we believe that success is determined by an ingrained level of ability as opposed to resilience and hard work, we will be brittle in the face of adversity."

—Joshua Waitzkin

You should understand by now that, if you have a fixed mindset, your belief is you either can or cannot do something well.

If you are certain that, for example, you are good at math, you might try to complete a difficult math problem.

But if the math problem is too complex to solve or if you can't solve it right away, you will give up, perhaps thinking that it's just too darn hard or maybe impossible to solve.

On the other hand, if you have a growth mindset, you'll continue working on the problem. You are certain that, with enough time and effort, and maybe even with some help from a mentor or teacher, you can learn how to solve the problem.

For people with a fixed mindset, the struggle is painful, because it shows them they aren't special. When presented with a challenge they haven't done well on in the past, they will generally try to avoid trying to do "it" at all costs.

On the other hand, for people with a growth mindset, the struggle is pleasurable. While it can make them uncomfortable for a while, they are certain that with effort they can succeed. They see a challenge as something that stretches them and helps them to grow.

Challenges make them feel good.

An excellent example of this mindset is Josh Waitzkin. Josh is one of the most highly skilled chess masters of all time.

He is also a world champion in Tai Chi Push Hands. He has led the U.S. Push Hands Team to several world titles.

Additionally, he is a black belt in Brazilian Jiu-Jitsu.

Because he was so good at playing chess, when he was young, he was compared to one of the finest chess players of all time, Bobby Fischer. He was so good, in fact, that he was the model for the protagonist in the 1993 movie *Searching for Bobby Fischer*.[6]

At age 6, his father, Fred Waitzkin, began teaching Josh how to play chess. Later he regularly played at the Marshall Chess Club on 10th Street.

In 1983, he discovered that people played chess in Washington Square. Washington Square had its share of chess hustlers, such as Vincent (Vinnie) Livermore and Israel (the Sheriff) Zilber.

Zilber had a rating of over 2400 for chess completion and was considered an International Master. In 1952, he won the Latvian Championship by defeating the world champion Mikhail Tal.

Also for a time, Grandmaster Roman Dzindzichashvili played chess at Washington Square. There were many great players to test his skills with.

---

[6] Paramount Pictures. (Based on the book by Fred Waitzkin, Josh's father.)

From these meetings, Josh believed he had the skills to enter chess championships.

In the spring of 1984, Josh was playing at the National Elementary Chess Championship in Syracuse, New York.

He lost in the seventh round.

He says that losing the National Chess championship was the best thing that ever happened to him.

Why?

Because the loss taught him the lesson that he wasn't special.

The loss taught Josh to change his fixed mindset of "being talented" into a growth mindset of "I need to work to get better." Since his defeat, he earned the title of National Master, and, at age 16, became an International Master.

Josh learned that to achieve the things he wanted, he needed to be willing to put in the work.

Josh provides us an excellent model of how to develop a growth mindset. Like Josh, all you have to do is stop thinking that you, or anybody else, is special.

Moving from Fixed to Flexible

For most of recorded history, we have been measuring intelligence. In fact, Chinese Emperor Ta Yu, better known as Yu the Great (from the 2000s BCE) reportedly used intelligence testing to hire, promote or fire his government's officials.

Intelligence testing still goes on today with teachers, psychologists, social scientists, employers, and doctors using tests like the Stanford-Binet Test, Weschler Scales, and Scholastic Assessment Test (SAT) to determine our mental abilities. The results these tests give tell us how high we'll climb in our world.

When I was growing up, these tests were definitive. They were how we were judged as students.

They measured how smart you were or were not.

They predicted how well you would do in school, at your job, and in other types of academic endeavors. There was no getting around them.

It was that simple.

Then Carol Dweck, a psychology professor and researcher from Stanford University, came along. Her research found that this simply wasn't the case.

She explains her findings in depth in her book *Mindset: The New Psychology of Success*.[7]

Professor Dweck found that a person's ability to learn wasn't a function of their test scores but rather of how they approached learning. She showed us that you could approach learning from either a fixed or a growth mindset.

This resonated profoundly with me because in both martial arts and NLP, we learn that our abilities aren't fixed, but rather can grow thorough trial and error. We can then utilize the feedback we receive to improve.

Failing at Hoops

With a fixed mindset, you believe that either you can or you cannot. Soon you won't try things because you are afraid of failing.

Social scientists call this the fear of failure.

John Atkinson, a Stanford University psychologist, began studying the fear of failure in the 1960s. His experiments gave children reward-based tasks to determine their motivation. This is described in depth in the 1969 book *Fear of Failure*.[8]

First, they observed the children. Then they divided them into two groups depending on their behavior.

[7] 2007, Ballantine Books.
[8] Birney, R.C., Burdick, H. & Teevan, R.C. (1969). New York: Van Nostrand- Reinhold Co.

The first group had a "need for achievement" attitude, wanting to improve. These children would keep trying because they wanted to perform at a higher level.

In contrast, the second group's focus was to avoid even the remotest possibility of public humiliation when they failed to accomplish the task. Atkinson named this phenomenon the "fear of failure."

To measure motivation, Atkinson had the children play a game where they would toss a hoop over a peg from a measured distance. They earned more points the farther they stood from the peg.

Those children who had a "need for achievement" stood a challenging but realistic distance from the peg. If they missed the peg, they would practice improving their technique or try concentrating better.

The children in the "fear of failure" group would behave one of two predictable ways. They either stood right next to the peg, making it impossible to fail, or at such a distance that it would have been pure luck if they succeeded.

It's easy to understand why they would stand so close—it was impossible to fail. But why would they stand so far away?

Atkinson theorized that those who stood so far back believed that it was impossible to put the hoop around the peg. Standing far away disguised their fear of failure.

When they stood far away, they could tell the other children that they hadn't failed due to lack of trying, but rather had tried their best and didn't succeed because they took greater risks. This allowed them to justify their behavior while successfully, at least in their minds, hiding their fear of failure.

This is a classic example of a fixed mindset. These children believed, for some reason, that they could only be marginally good at hoop throwing. No amount of practice was going to make them better.

Their fixed mindsets made them so afraid of failure and being humiliated or laughed at that they avoided trying altogether. In fact, when asked to participate again, many of the children in the fear of failure group would act out, becoming disruptive, saying things like, "I really didn't want to play anyway."

A few even tried to stop the other children from playing.

A fear of failure mindset brings up negative feelings, thoughts, and emotions about you and your abilities when you make mistakes or have setbacks. These "failure" events become barriers that continually block you, preventing you from ever achieving the outcomes you desire. They limit your ability to look for solutions and, ultimately, to perform.

With this fixed mindset, you can't learn anything useful from your actions. You only see "failure."

On the other hand, a growth mindset allows you to see mistakes and problems as what they are: learning experiences.

Look at it this way. Throughout your life, the only way you've learned anything is by doing it wrong the first time. From learning to walk to learning to write a complete sentence, we all do it "wrong" at first.

But this is how all of us learn. Instead of failures, mistakes are simply stepping-stones to the right answer. They provide feedback.

This is what Dweck observed and what led her to conclude that, as long as we maintain the growth mindset that the children in the need for achievement group exhibited, our possibilities can and will remain limitless.

The Plastic Mind

Carol Dweck's mindset theory allows us to see limitations as what they truly are: illusions. What's even more interesting is that neuroscientists have come to the same conclusion, at least about the brain's ability to continue to adapt and grow throughout our lives. Our past illusions about its ability to grow are being swept away.

In the book *The Brain That Changes Itself: Stories of Personal Triumph from the Frontiers of Brain Science*,[9] Dr. Norman Doidge explains that the mechanical model of the brain is no longer accurate. Dr. Doidge illustrates this through several very interesting studies on people and animals.

These studies show that our brains have incredible plasticity. Study after study shows that stimulating the brain increases the number of neuron branches, blood flow, and, in turn, brain size. What's really exciting, at least for adults, is that this doesn't end at childhood, as was thought in the past.

Your brain can continue to grow throughout your lifetime.

In his book, Dr. Doidge refers to Barbara Arrowsmith, the creator and director of Arrowsmith School and Arrowsmith Program. She is also the author of the internationally best-selling book *The Woman Who Changed Her Brain*.[10]

As a child, although she was brilliant in some areas, Arrowsmith couldn't understand concepts, ideas, and relationships. Additionally she was very clumsy and uncoordinated.

In her book, she refers to the left side of her body as an "alien being" that she couldn't control. She also couldn't understand the sensations her body received on her left side.

Because she didn't understand those sensations, she constantly bumped into things with the left side of her body. Then, after bumping into something, she didn't understand where the pain she was feeling was coming from.

As a child, she was diagnosed with a "mental block" that she visualized as a real wooden block in her head. This vision,

---

[9] 2007, Viking Press.
[10] 2012, Free Press.

and the feelings she had about her disability, resulted in a deep depression.

In eighth grade she tried to commit suicide. She said wanted to end her struggles and their accompanying pain.

Later in her life, and with her parents' encouragement, she decided to try to figure out what was wrong with her. To do this, she went off to college and majored in psychology.

In 1977, Barbara read about a Russian soldier who had the same symptoms as her. The only difference were his symptoms were a result of a bullet entering his brain.

This led Barbara to begin looking for clues to help her "fix" herself. Her search uncovered the studies of Mark Rosenzweig, an American research psychologist who studied rats.

In his studies, Dr. Rosenzweig had found that, in a stimulated environment, a rat's brain could continue to develop physiologically, no matter the age or damage.

Dr. Rosenzweig's studies inspired Arrowsmith to create her own exercises that would stimulate her brain. After a few months of using her exercises, her ability to read and understand philosophy, something she had never been able to do before, increased dramatically.

Ms. Arrowsmith saw this as "neuroplasticity in action, the brain changing and growing as a result of stimulation."

The brain was actually plastic!

We can look at this as evidence that the capacity of our brains is not fixed. That, if we look at experiences as learning situations and continue to give ourselves the right feedback, our abilities can continue to grow and flourish throughout our lives.

But this can be hard for many to believe.

Why?

Because of a scary voice inside of you that's been talking to you for your entire life. Your zombie voice.

Chapter 28

Your Zombie Voice

"Most of the important things in the world have been accomplished by people who have kept on trying when there seemed to be no hope at all."

—Dale Carnegie

After a young reporter asked Thomas Edison, "How does it feel to have failed so many times to make a light bulb?" he replied, "I have not failed. I've just found 10,000 ways that won't work."

This is the growth mindset in action.

Thomas Edison could respond this way because he had learned how to tame his self-talk, that zombie voice inside us all.

All of us have internal self-talk, or a continuous conversation going on inside our minds. Often, this conversation goes something like this:

"Okay, you've got to get this project done, where should you start?"

Why are you asking me, I don't want to do this project. I'd rather be at the beach surfing!"

"There's no surfing today."

"Why not? You're a lot better at surfing than this stuff. In fact, you'll probably just mess this up like you did the last time when Mary had to bail you out."

"I can do this, and, by the way, she didn't bail me out. She just helped me make a few tweaks to the presentation."

"You know you're not good enough. Why don't you just pack up your stuff and go surfing? It'll be a lot easier!"

On it goes.

Maybe your zombie voice doesn't sound exactly like this, but, unless you've done a lot of work to quiet this conversation, it's probably regularly telling you a lot of negative things about you. Things you picked from your parents, peers, and teacher. Some you've even told yourself.

While you might tell yourself you don't believe some of these things, they still come up. They nag at your constantly.

You know what the voice says. It says things like:

"You're not good enough,"

"Why does this always happen to me?"

"I'm just not lucky," and other extremely disempowering thoughts and feelings.

The fact is, your zombie voice is always with you, and, unless you learn how to control it, it's going to hold you back for the rest of your life.

How?

By affecting what you believe you can and cannot accomplish.

Your zombie voice will block you from ever getting into the zone.

Eddie the Eagle

An excellent example of how the zombie voice can affect us comes from the movie *Eddie the Eagle*.[11]

---

[11] 2015, Marv Films, Studio Babelsberg and Saville Productions.

Eddie the Eagle is a true story about an extremely tenacious man, Eddie Edwards. Played by Taron Egerton, Eddie wants to be an Olympic athlete. In fact, throughout his life, Eddie's primary goal has been to compete in the Olympics. Although he qualifies to be a part of the Olympic ski team, the British Olympic officials reject him because they feel he is not a "proper" representative of the British Olympic team.

This rejection leads to a new decision, to become a ski jumper. This is in spite of the fact that the United Kingdom hadn't participated in ski jumping for over sixty years.

However, there's a problem. The UK doesn't have a ski jumping facility.

Refusing to be dissuaded from his goal, Eddie decides to go to a training facility in Garmisch- Partenkirchen, Germany. His experience is anything but gentle. In fact, he accumulates numerous bumps and bruises and has at least one visit to the hospital.

Eventually he receives guidance from former Olympian jumper and current drunken snow groomer, Bronson Peary played by Hugh Jackman. To make a long story short, with Peary's coaching, Eddie qualifies to be part of the British Olympic team as their one and only ski jumper and off to the Olympics he goes.

Olympic completion has two jump heights. These are 70 and 90 meters.

Eddie enters the Olympics with the idea that he will only jump from 70 meters. But, after completing his 70-meter jump, Eddie makes a last-minute decision to enter the 90-meter jump competition.

Now this presents Eddie with another problem. He's never jumped from 90 meters before. This jump is going to be not only an Olympic first but it's going to be his personal first.

As we watch, Eddie rides the elevator and eventually reaches the top, seemingly a mile high in the air. Sitting atop the summit

Wil Dieck   151

that's as tall as a football field is long (300 feet), voices from his past start to speak to him, wafting through his brain.

He hears zombie voices, like his father telling him he would never be an Olympic athlete. He hears the Olympic official telling him he wasn't Olympics material.

Negative voices from the past fill his mind. These voices nearly keep him from jumping as he temporarily freezes in place.

Of course, it didn't end like this. If it had, they probably wouldn't have made a movie about him.

Through pure willpower, built over years of stubborn effort, Eddie calms those voices and controls his self-talk. This allows him to complete the jump and enter the history books as Britain's premier ski jumper, even though he is in last place at the Olympics.

This only happened because Eddie was able to turn off his zombie voices.

Are You Really Listening?

Without a doubt, you have these zombie voices talking to you too. These conversations are happening all the time, but if you don't pay attention to them, you won't even be aware of how they are affecting you.

This is because you're not really listening and, most likely, these conversations are being automatically generated by your lizard brain. Because you're not listening, you don't consciously hear them, but they affect you anyway as your fight or flight response is activated, over and over again.

Unconscious thoughts like, "Look how poorly my team is performing. I must be a terrible manager," or, "That decision really sucked. I must really suck!" can, and probably do, make you feel unsure, uncertain and unsafe.

Why do you feel unsafe?

Your uncertainty activates your fight or flight response and, as you discovered earlier, your mammalian brain begins to operate less and less efficiently. Not only do these thoughts make you feel bad, they hijack your thinking.

As a result, your prefrontal cortex starts shutting down, making you act more and more irrationally.

This is your zombie mind in action.

Your Zombie Mind in Action

Here's how your zombie mind works.

Let's say you set a goal to increase your sales by fifty percent. Your zombie mind tells you, "Who are you kidding? You're always making pie in the sky promises to yourself. You'll never be able to increase your sales by fifty percent!"

While your rational logical mind helped you create what you thought to be a realistic goal, your zombie mind cuts your legs out from under you. And here's what's key: you can't do something that your zombie mind thinks it can't. While you may struggle for a while to accomplish this outcome, there will come a point where you just give up.

Your inner zombie has taken over.

But it doesn't have to be this way. You can tame your inner zombie.

We'll look at how you can do this next.

Chapter 29

Taming Your Inner Zombie

"He who has power over himself has power over his greatest enemy."

—Matshona Dhliwayo

An old Cherokee sits down with his grandson to teach him about life.

"A fight is going on inside me," he said to the boy. "It is a terrible fight and it is between two wolves. One is evil. He is anger, envy, sorrow, regret, greed, arrogance, self-pity, guilt, resentment, inferiority, lies, false pride, superiority, and ego."

The young boy looks intently at his grandfather and begins to speak when his grandfather holds up his hand. The boy remains silent.

The grandfather continues, "The other is good. He is joy, peace, love, hope, serenity, humility, kindness, benevolence, empathy, generosity, truth, compassion, and faith."

Watching his grandson for a nearly a minute, the grandfather looks in his grandson's eyes and says, "The same fight is going on inside you and inside every other person, too."

For about a minute, the grandson remains silent, thinking to himself. Finally, he asks his grandfather, "Which wolf will win?"

The old Cherokee simply replied, "The one you feed."

The grandfather is right. Your thoughts can be your own worst enemy. That is, if you let them.

What Kind of Wolf Are You Feeding?

As the grandfather pointed out to his grandson, learning to control your thoughts is how you win the inner battle.

For many people, the evil wolf is winning. Every day these people feed this evil wolf with their negative thoughts.

While there are many more to choose from, the following are the three most common negative thoughts:

"I'm Not Good Enough"

"I'm Not Smart Enough"

I Don't Belong Here"

The best way to overcome the power of these negative thoughts is through a process called reframing. Learning to reframe these self-critical thoughts is how you control which wolf wins.

Thais is what you're going to learn next.

Reframing Your Inner Critic

"For any single thing of importance, there are multiple reasons."

—M. Scott Peck

You can create greater peace, confidence and a more positive outlook by learning how to manage your thoughts. This is the first step of being able to drop into the zone.

How can you learn to manage your thoughts?

By using what I call Five R Process.

The 5 R Process

There are five steps in the 5 R process. These are:

1. **Recognize**
2. **Record**
3. **Remind**
4. **Replace**
5. **Repeat**

Let's look at these five steps, one at a time.

Recognize

For many people, the inner zombie is winning. The worst part is you might not even be aware of what your inner zombie is telling you.

To tame your inner zombie you must first become aware of those thoughts and then capture them. This is the recognize step.

To be aware of your zombie mind's thoughts, you have to be able to recognize them in the moment. You need to see them for what they are—zombie thoughts—as they come up.

You need to pay attention and listen to what your inner zombie is telling you.

The good news is, if you have been doing the exercises so far, you are already doing this back in Chapter 20.

As a reminder, the process is when a disempowering thought comes up, recognize it for what it is: a limiting belief.

You must be aware of it!

This is the only way you can remedy it.

Don't try to gloss over it and don't try to pretend it doesn't exist. Listen, recognize and the record it.

This is the next step, and if you are doing the exercise from Chapter 20, you are already doing this.

Record

The next step is to record what your self-critic is telling you.

Write these thoughts down in the moment, as soon as they come up. Again, you should have started doing this after Chapter 20. You can use whatever you want to record them; your smart phone, an audio recorder or just a simple notepad will do.

Then we're going to add a new step. In the evening, you're going to transfer your self-critical thoughts into your journal so you can analyze them.

Review

Now that you've recorded what your zombie mind is telling you, the third step is to put these thoughts and feelings into your journal. As you do this, you'll probably discover that many of these same thoughts pop up, over and over again.

When reviewing these thoughts, ask yourself:

When did this thought rear its ugly head?

Was it a certain time of day, after a conversation with a certain person, or after doing a certain task?"

How often do you have this thought?

Does it come up regularly?

What does it sound like?

Where is it coming from?

Whose voice do you hear? (We'll talk more about these last three in a minute.)

Being aware of your triggers will help you prepare for them in the future.

Replace

You've captured what your zombie voice is telling you and you've analyzed it. Now it's time to do the fourth step: replacing the disempowering thought with an optimistic one.

Before you move on to the mechanics of this exercise, I want you to make a list of your greatest accomplishments.

Here's short list to get you thinking:

- Finding the love of your life.
- Being on a winning team.
- Winning a competition.
- Graduating from high school or college.
- Serving in the military.
- Getting a promotion for doing a great job.

Of course, you can put whatever you want on your list.

Get your journal and do this now!

Okay you're back. You did do the exercise, right?

When a negative thought comes up, go to your list of achievements. This will remind you that you have been successful in the past.

Now, let's say the thought, "I'll never be able to increase my sales by fifty percent" suddenly appears in your zombie mind.

Instead of thinking of this thought as real, look at your list of accomplishments for a sales success you've had. If it's not there, search for a sales success you've had in your past and write it in your list.

Look, unless you're brand new to sales, you've obviously had successes. Maybe you closed a big deal, or improved sales last year by twenty-five percent.

This is your reminder.

You're going to use this reminder to replace the thought, "I'll never be able to increase my sales by fifty percent" with "Last year I increased sales by twenty- five percent. I can double that success this year."

Another example might be after you slip on your health program. Instead of letting your zombie voice keep telling you, "I'm not good enough," find an accomplishment where you have persevered in the past.

Remember times when you *were* "good enough."

This might be when you graduated from college or when you completed a complicated project at work. You're turning these memories of past successes into replacement phrases.

Repeat

Now that you've gone through the first four steps, you're going to use the fifth step—repeat, to make your optimistic thought your habitual one.

In the future, when the thought, "You'll never be able to increase your sales by fifty percent!" comes up, you repeat your replacement phrase to yourself.

(You can go to https://tinyurl.com/Mindful-Mastery-Journal to get your FREE interactive journal especially designed for this book.)

You'll do this in combination with the final part of the convergence triad. your state.

We'll talk more about this more a little later.

Chapter 30

Defining Your Zombie Voice

"If you're not willing to take the actions to change your situation - in other words, if you're willing to put up with your situation - then whether you like it or not, that is the life you have chosen."

—Gary John Bishop

or some people, Gary John Bishop's quote can be hard to read. Why?

Because deep down inside they know this is true. We have the ability to choose how we talk to ourselves. This allows us to change the way we think about ourselves.

The problem is most people don't bother.

You've decided to be different. You've begun paying attention to what your zombie voice is telling you.

But now that you're listening and making note of what your zombie voice is saying, you might be wondering why you've never noticed it before.

You might be wondering, "What has my zombie voice been telling me up to now?"

No matter what the conversation has been, you probably won't be able to eliminate it, but you, like Eddie the Eagle, can learn to take control of it.

Breaking Down Your Zombie Talk

Let's examine a hypothetical zombie thought.

Maybe, as you work, you're hearing, "I'm a phony. I don't belong here."

By the way, you are not alone. Many very accomplished people feel this way. But even though many people feel this way, it doesn't make the thought any less painful or impactful.

The way you're going to learn how to control this voice is by going through and identifying the submodalities of the voice you're hearing. (If you're interested in learning more about modalities and submodalities, check out Chapter 2 of my book *Secrets of the Black Belt Mindset.*

(You can go to https://tinyurl.com/Mindful-Mastery-Journal to get your FREE interactive journal especially designed for this book.)

The first thing I want you to identify is whose voice it is talking to you.

While it may be your own voice, I want you to really listen to it. What you may find is that it's the voice of your old football or dance coach, your father or mother, or some other significant person from your past.

Take the time to really listen to this voice.

You want to be certain of whose voice you're hearing. Once you've identified the voice, write down in your journal whose voice it is.

Now that you've identified who the voice represents, where, in relationship to you, is it coming from?

Is the voice coming from inside or outside of you? Write down in your journal where the voice is coming from.

Don't worry about why just yet. We'll cover why you're doing all of this in a little while.

If the voice is coming from outside of you, identify the direction it's coming from.

Is it behind you, in front of you, or to your left or right?

Is it above you or below you?

Write down in your journal where in space, relative to you, the voice is coming from.

If the voice is coming from inside you, where inside you is it coming from?

Is it inside your head? If it is inside your head, is it in the front, the back, on the left, or on the right; at the top or bottom of your skull?

Is it inside your body? Where? In your heart?

Is it in your stomach? If it's in your stomach, is it in the center of your stomach or is it at the bottom or the top?

Maybe it's coming from your big toe. While this is highly unlikely, it could be.

Where exactly in your head or body is the voice coming from? Write the exact spot in your journal.

What's the volume of that voice? Is it very loud or so soft you can barely hear it or something in between? Write in your journal how loud it is.

What is the pitch of that voice? The pitch is the frequency of how deep or high the sound is. Do you hear a low pitch, a high pitch or something in between? Describe the pitch of that voice in your journal.

While there are many other ways to describe a sound (again, see *Secrets of the Black Belt Mindset*), for simplicity's sake, we're going to stick to these. But if you'd like to add more submodalities, by all means, add more.

This exercise should have given you a fairly accurate idea of where your zombie voice is coming from and what it sounds like.

Now, the next thing you need to know is how to control it.

Adjusting Your Zombie Voice

As Eddie the Eagle listened to those voices atop the 90-meter jump, he had a choice: he could allow them to hijack his dream or he could decide to take control.

Of course, Eddie took control, dropped into the zone and jumped into history.

So can you.

Taking control doesn't mean eliminating the voice. This is because it's simply not possible to eliminate it.

The voice is and has probably been a part of you for a long time. The voice can also try to prod you into doing things that need being done, For example, if you have a destructive habit, like smoking or drinking too much, the voice may try to remind you that you should change your behavior.

Taking control doesn't mean trying to argue with the voice.

Have you ever tried to convince somebody to do something by arguing with them? How has that worked for you?

I'm guessing that you've never been able to argue someone over to your side.

The question is how can you take control of your zombie voice? The answer is by making small shifts in how you hear the voice. How do you make those shifts?

By controlling the submodalities of that voice.

Let's say your voice is telling you, "You're not good enough." Instead of ignoring the voice or trying to silence it, listen to it.

Whose voice is telling you this?

If it's your voice, try turning the voice into a cartoon character's voice or a voice that makes you laugh. Note how this changes the voice's effect on you.

As you make each change, write down how changing whose voice it is affected you in your journal.

Now, let's work on the location of the voice.

If the voice was inside your head, try moving it outside and behind you about 5 or 10 feet.

Next, move the voice out 25 feet, then 100 feet.

Now move the voice to your right by 5 or 10 feet, then 50 feet, then 100 feet.

Do the same thing to your left.

Try moving it out in front of you, 5, 10, 50, and then 100 feet. Move it down by your feet, then move it above your head.

Now leave the voice inside you but move it to your elbow, your knee, or your big toe.

Notice how moving the voice changes its effect on you.

Write down how changing where the voice is located in the space around you or moving it to different places within your body affects you in your journal.

If the voice was outside of you, note where it is in space and then try pushing it further away, again by 5, 10, 25, and then 100 feet. If it's above you, move it below you.

We often associate a voice above us with an authority figure, like our parents, so if you move it below, you may start to feel in control.

Now move the voice inside you, again to your elbow, your knee, or your big toe.

Notice how moving the voice changes how it affects you.

Write down how changing where the voice is located in the space around you or moving it to different places within your body affects you in your journal.

Now let's turn the volume up and down on your zombie control console.

If the voice is exceptionally soft and forcing you to pay close attention to it, try increasing the volume.

If the voice is very loud, try turning the volume down.

Notice how turning the control volume of your control console up and down changes how it affects you.

Write down how controlling the volume affects you in your journal.

Finally, let's work on changing the pitch of the voice.

If it's a deep, bass voice, try changing it to a high soprano voice. If it's a high voice, try changing it to a scratchy voice.

Play with the pitch and note how it affects you in your journal.

By now, you should have written a full set of operating instructions for your zombie voice control console.

Now that you have your instructions, you can get them to work for you.

Chapter 31

What Kind of Tattoo
Do You Have?

"When you change the way you look at things, the things you look at change."

—Wayne Dyer

t happened in the mid-1970s while hanging around Pinky's Tattoo Parlor in Hong Kong while on R&R. Two friends had decided to get tattoos, so I tagged along with them.

One had a butterfly tattooed on the back of his shoulder. Well, it was the 70s after all.

The other one got a tattoo of USDA Choice on his right butt cheek. That was funny at the time.

Today he's well over 60. I wonder how that tattoo looks now?

OH, wrong image!

Let's get back to Pinky's.

While my friends were getting their tattoos, someone working there handed me a beer. Of course, the beer was to put me in a state of mind that was open to getting a tattoo somewhere on my body.

As I sipped my beer, I watched one British sailor get a battle-ship tattooed on his chest with guns blazing. Another was having Bruce Lee with nunchakus swirling around his head tattooed on his back.

Tired of watching these men being turned into somewhat bloody, living art, I began to look at the large display case filled with tattoo patterns to choose from.

There was one of Popeye the sailor flexing his biceps. Another was a large heart with an arrow through it and space to put whatever name you wanted.

Perusing row after row of tattoos, my eyes finally landed on a tattoo of an anchor with "Born to Lose" scrolled across the middle.

An old Chinese gentleman had been following me as I walked around the display case, so I asked him, "Do people really get this tattoo?"

He took a big drag off his cigarette, squinted, exhaled a large cloud of smoke in my face, tapped his forehead and said, "Before tattoo on body, tattoo in mind."

Do you remember that TV show, *Kung-Fu*, where David Carradine starred as Kwai Chang Caine, a Shaolin monk, traveling through the American Old West?

Often Caine would have a flashback where the blind Master Po would give the young Caine philosophical advice. Well for me, that was a real Master Po philosophical experience.

It was also something I'll never forget.

So, what does this have to do with you?

You, like many other people, may have anchored this, or something like it, in your mind.

You want to know the worst part of this?

You may be repeating, "Born to lose" to yourself, over and over again, without even being aware of it.

This is where many of your problems begin.

Why?

It's because everything in your life started with a thought.

It's your thoughts that guide your actions.

Repeat those actions enough times, they become habits.

What you do habitually controls your focus and, eventually, becomes your destiny.

This is why what that old Chinese gentleman told me was so important. Life will give you what you habitually focus on. So, if you focus on the tattoo, "Born to Lose," you will become a loser.

But by changing your thinking, you can change your focus. This change in focus will alter your habitual actions.

Now you are moving in a different direction.

This is how you take control of your destiny and how learning how to tame your zombie voice can help.

By learning how to control your thoughts, you can begin to focus on taking the right actions. These are the actions will help you complete the goals you need to do so you can live the life you want to live.

Taming Your Zombie Voice

Since your zombie voice interferes with your beliefs, wouldn't it be a good idea to learn how to tame it?

The great news is that it's not nearly as hard as you might think, as long as you've completed your zombie voice self-assessment.

You have completed your zombie voice self-assessment, haven't you?

Let's say your zombie voice tells you, "You're such a failure!"

While that sounds harsh, most of us have a thought like that, or a very similar one, thrown at us at least every once in a while.

This is especially true when things don't go exactly as we've planned.

To counter the voice, you need to be prepared.

Just as a black belt practices their techniques over and over again, you need to rehearse your response to your zombie voice's negative messages.

This is how you prevent getting an anchor with "Born to Lose" tattooed in your mind.

The first thing you need to do to prepare is be aware of that thought.

You're already able to do this because you've been paying attention to your zombie voice and writing down what it says in your journal.

Next, you've been playing with that thought by changing whose voice it is, changing the location, the volume, and the pitch.

Remember to have fun with this and note in your journal which methods best dim your zombie voice's effect on you.

The final preparation step is to continue to create and use optimistic replacement phrases.

Using the example of the thought, "You're a failure!" when you make a mistake, you might write something along the lines of, "Mistakes are opportunities for me to learn and grow. Learning and growing allows me to become the best I can possibly be!"

Then, after you say your positive self-affirmation, pump your fists into the air and say something like, "Yes!" or, "Awesome!"

We'll talk more about how to do this later.

Dimming the Zombie Voice

Okay, you've gone through the preparation stage.

You have heard the voice and recorded it in your self-talk journal. You have played around with shifting how the voice appears to you.

You've created positive, countering, replacement phrases.

You have practiced saying your replacement phrases

You are now fully prepared to take on your zombie voice.

Imagine it's the middle of the afternoon and you have just uncovered a mistake you've made in a report that is due in a couple of hours.

Your zombie voice taps you on the shoulder and says, "You're such a failure."

Here's what you're going to do:

1. Acknowledge the zombie voice.

2. Shift the voice in a way that dims it or makes it less (the way you've been rehearsing).

3. Say your positive affirmation aloud. For this example, we'll imagine you say, "Mistakes are opportunities for me to learn and grow. Learning and growing allows me to become the best I can possibly be!"

4. Pump your arms and hands in the air and say, "Awesome!" or whatever positive reinforcement you've chosen.

We'll look at this more in the next chapter.

You are no longer allowing your zombie voice to control your beliefs. Instead, you are now controlling what you say to yourself.

This makes it much easier for you to drop into the zone.

Widening Your Search

I hope that what you've discovered in this chapter is that you're not special, that your abilities aren't fixed, that your brain, like everyone else's in the world, can continue to adapt and grow as long as you continue to be willing to take on new challenges.

This allows you to learn from your experiences (pessimistic people would call these mistakes or failures).

You've discovered that, by adopting the growth mindset and looking at unsuccessful attempts as feedback, you can widen your search pattern and expand your beliefs.

No longer do you ask, "Why did I fail?" but instead, "What did I learn?"

This allows you to you understand that if what you are doing isn't working, it doesn't mean you have failed. It's just you, like Thomas Edison, just haven't achieved the result you want.

As Carol Dweck so elegantly puts it, you haven't achieved what you've set out to do - **YET**.

To succeed, you just need to look for different solutions that bring you to the outcome you desire.

You now understand that the light switch on the wall is actually a dimmer switch that allows you to control your zombie voice.

You are now using it to your full advantage and taking charge of your beliefs.

You are creating the right kind of mental tattoos, ones that reflect who you really are.

Now let's take a look at how to take charge of your state.

Chapter 32

Wild Thing

"A calm mind brings inner strength and self-confidence, so that's very important for good health."

—Dalai Lama

*L*et's review. Your brain has a wild side. It's called the limbic system. It's also often referred to as the lizard brain. This is because of how much it has in common with a lizard's brain.

This primitive part of your brain is the seat of emotion, addiction, mood, and many other mental and emotional processes. These are processes like the acute stress response, also known as your fight, flight or freeze response.

Most of the time, people refer to the acute stress response simply as the fight or flight response.

The acute stress response activates your sympathetic nervous system. The sympathetic nervous system gets your body ready to fight or flee.

While the fight or flight response is great for handling real emergencies, like defending yourself against a grizzly bear or an angry kangaroo, in our modern world it can be, and often is, activated in situations where it's not needed or even useful.

For example, let's say you have an important meeting in a city 350 miles away. You book your flight, pack your overnight bag, and drive to the airport. As you go through airport security, members of TSA check your bag and your body.

Next, you are bumped and jostled by other soon-to-be passengers scurrying to catch their flights. Then, barring delays, you squeeze your way onto a narrow metal tube that is going to take you from zero to somewhere between 130 and 155 knots per hour (150–180 mph) in 30 to 35 seconds, You push your bag into the overhead compartment, slightly bumping your head as you do and then sit in your rather uncomfortable chair.

If you don't hit any turbulence, the flight itself can be fairly calming. It might even lull you to sleep, that is if there are no crying babies or two people who just met babbling about their deepest secrets in the row right behind you.

Finally, the plane starts to descend, but to save fuel for the airline (pilots will tell you that they do this all the time), the pilot makes a quick descent starting at about 250 knots (280 mph) and then slowing to a reasonable speed, hitting the ground with a jostling bump. The brakes are applied and your head and body compress into the seat as the plane slows to a driving speed.

Now, as you throttle to the gate, people start getting up and pulling their luggage from the overhead bins. The cabin fills with noise and everyone rushes to get off the plane.

You scurry to the pickup point and find your Uber driver, who speeds you to your hotel. You wait for your turn to check in, and then you take the elevator to your room. It's time to go over your notes and get ready for your meeting.

You're ready to go, right?

Wrong!

Your lizard brain identifies all of these events as possible threats, putting your fight or flight system on alert. No wonder when you get to your destination you feel tired, out of sorts, and your body doesn't operate the way it should.

While you may not be in full-on panic mode, you brain is definitely not operating optimally. This could make all the difference in the world for the deal you're about to try to close.

So what can you do to counter the effects of your lizard brain's reaction? You can use your parasympathetic nervous system to keep it in check.

Taking Back Control from Your Lizard Brain

Your parasympathetic nervous system includes the processes your body uses to control homeostasis. This system is also called your rest and digest response.

Homeostasis means keeping things constant. Its root comes from two Greek words: homeo, meaning similar, and stasis, meaning stable.

What this means for us is our body composition, including our temperature, salt, and potassium levels, stays fairly constant or stable over time.

For example, if you go outside on a hot day and run around, your body temperature will shoot up and your parasympathetic nervous system will send a signal from your mind to your body to sweat. This cools you down and keeps your temperature within its normal range. This is homeostasis in action.

The other main function of your parasympathetic nervous system is to conserve energy by slowing the heart rate, increasing intestinal and glandular activity, and relaxing the sphincter muscles in the gastrointestinal tract. This response is also known as the rest and digest response.

It's called rest and relax because it helps us feel relaxed. It is the exact opposite of the acute stress response.

After you go through a stressful event where your acute stress response kicks in, your parasympathetic nervous system is supposed to take over and return your body to homeostasis.

It does this by slowing your heart rate and respiration, bringing blood back into your intestines, and relaxing your muscles. The problem is that, because of the environment we live in, homeostasis can be hard to reach.

Since you haven't been able to relax, you're still on alert, and your body and brain, especially your prefrontal cortex, are affected.

What does this mean?

It means that your brain is operating at less than its optimal level.

What can you do to bring your brain back into homeostasis?

You need to engage your parasympathetic nervous.

How?

By taking a breather.

The Art of Taking a Breather

Have you ever been practicing a sport or doing hard, physical labor when someone says, "Let's take a breather"?

Even if you haven't, you've most likely heard the saying before. Its purpose is to remind us to take a break.

The "breather" allows our muscles to relax, which helps our heart rate and breathing slow down. Since practicing a sport or doing hard physical work can tax your cardiovascular system, taking a breather helps your mind and body return to, or at least move toward, homeostasis.

While some people believe you only have to take a breather when you're doing something physical, it's important to take a break no matter what kind of work you're doing.

This is especially important if you're doing "brain work."

Scientists have established that your brain uses up to 20 percent of your body's total energy. This is more energy than any of your other organs.

If it makes sense to take a breather after hard physical labor, doesn't it make sense to do the same when you're overworked and stressed and your lizard brain is clamoring to take over?

When you take a breather, you begin to activate your parasympathetic nervous system. This helps to bring your body and mind back to an optimal level of operation.

But to be useful, you have to take your breather correctly. You have to practice the same type of breathing taught to martial artists, yoga practitioners, and athletes from just about any sport you can think of. This type of breathing is called diaphragmatic breathing. This is the type of breathing we talked about in Chapter 21.

As you probably remember, when you breathe diaphragmatically, you are breathing into your abdomen. This is how we humans naturally breathe. If you watch babies, you'll see that their stomachs rise and fall as they breathe.

The same happens for most people when they are sleeping, meditating, in a hypnotic trance, or just deeply relaxed.

Breathing into your abdomen contracts your diaphragm, causing it to descend. When your diaphragm descends, it leaves a gap for your lungs to expand and fill with air; your stomach rises and falls as you breathe.

This engages your parasympathetic systems and brings your mind and body back into their natural homeostatic state.

This is the primary way Zen masters, black belts and anyone else disengage their lizard brain and get their body ready to drop into the zone.

If you use this process regularly, you won't have to worry about your lizard brain taking over.

Step by step, moment by moment, you'll take deep belly breaths as you pack your bag.

You'll breathe calmly as you drive to the airport.

You'll arrive calm and relaxed and you'll remain in a calm state during your cavity search. Well, maybe not so much there, but, barring the cavity search, you should arrive at your destination with a calm lizard brain and your mammalian brain operating at close to full capacity.

You've successfully put your body into a calm, powerful state. You're nearly ready to close that big deal.

Chapter 33

How to Find the Right Frame

"We must, however, acknowledge, as it seems to me, that man with all his noble qualities... still bears in his bodily frame the indelible stamp of his lowly origin."

—Charles Darwin

While it would be nice and simple if all you had to do were control your breathing pattern to tame your lizard brain, there's slightly more to it. You need to be able to find the right frame.

A frame, or frame of reference, is simply how you make sense of the information you take in from the world.

For example, let's say you are reading The *Amityville Horror.*[12] You are engrossed in a very scary scene, when suddenly you hear a loud noise coming from the back of the house.

The hairs on your neck stick up, your heart begins to race, and you might even reach for that old baseball bat you keep in the corner of your room. Your mind races, and images of the night

---

[12] Anson, J. (1977). Prentice Hall.

slasher appear as you wonder if somehow he's gotten into the back of your house.

Right now, your lizard brain has put you into a state of heightened alert. It is getting you ready to fight, freeze, or flee.

Instead, let's say you are reading a very funny part of *Bossypants*[13] when suddenly you hear that same strange noise from the back of your house.

You might think to yourself, "I wonder what the cat knocked over this time?" You go back to happily reading your book.

Because of your frame, how you made sense of the information, you were in a much more relaxed state. In this relaxed state, your mammalian brain was able to more accurately interpret the information about the noise, compare it to similar information you experienced in your past, and put it into a proper perspective.

You see, it was your perspective about the situation that told you whether the noise was the ominous night slasher coming to do you harm or just the cat.

Just like the noise, it's your perspective that you attained from your past experiences that allows you to make sense of the information you're taking in from the world around you, moment to moment.

Perspective results from how you look at something.

You can look at an object from one angle and it can give you one perspective, but from another angle, you get a completely different perspective.

This is exactly what happened with the six blind men who wanted to describe an elephant.

These six blind men lived together in a hut in rural India. One day, a little boy came running into the blind men's hut, shouting, "There's an elephant in the village!"

---

[13] Fey, T. (2011). Little Brown and Company.

The blind men, who had never seen an elephant (no pun intended), wanted to find out what an elephant looked like, so they all held hands and had the boy lead them to where the elephant calmly stood in the middle of the village.

The blind men surrounded the elephant. One put his hands on the trunk and said, "I know what the elephant looks like! It looks like the trunk of a tree!"

Putting his hands on one of the elephant's ears, another exclaimed, "No! The elephant looks like a big fan!"

A third put his hands on the elephant's legs and announced, "No, you're wrong! The elephant looks like the pillars of the temple."

Still another grabbed the tail and shouted, "What are you saying? The elephant is nothing like anything you've said. It looks like the branch of a tree!"

One put his hands against the side of the elephant saying, "No, the elephant looks like the walls of the temple!"

The one who was feeling the tusks said, "You are all wrong! The elephant looks like a sharp spear."

As the blind men argued, their shouting becoming louder and louder, disturbing everyone in the village. Their noise was annoying everyone.

Finally, the wise man of the village walked to where the blind men were arguing and shouted, "STOP!"

The blind men recognized his voice and stopped their bickering.

The wise man said, "Here's what you're going to do, you're going to rotate around the elephant."

At the wise man's insistence, the blind men shuffled from one spot to another, each time experiencing the elephant from a new angle. Of course, this allowed them to frame the elephant differently, giving each of them a new perspective of what an elephant looked like.

Much of the time, we're like the blind men; we only see one perspective. This is especially true when your zombie mind takes over.

You can change this.

You, like the blind men, can "see" better by framing your experience differently, giving yourself a new perspective.

To frame your perspective differently, you simply need to change your state.

Zombie Postures

Do you remember Al from back in Chapter 14?

He was the client who came into my office with his shoulders slumped and his eyes focused on the ground.

The reason I asked him if he had eaten was to understand how depressed he actually was. Since he had eaten breakfast, I figured he wasn't depressed with a big "D." This was good news.

I decided to show him a process that would transmute his state. By transmuting his state, he could frame what was going on differently.

This would give him a new perspective.

You can use this process too. All you have to do is smile. You can use this process any time you're feeling a little down.

Here's how it works:

First, think back to a time when you felt down and depressed with a little "d."

Maybe you botched a presentation to a big client or you didn't get "the" job.

Maybe it was a personal situation where you had an argument with a friend or your significant other and, in that moment, you felt down and in the dumps.

Whatever the situation, use your imagination to guide your posture. Let your shoulders slump and focus your eyes on the floor, the same way Al did.

Right now, the world may seem dim; sounds might seem muffled, your stomach could even feel upset.

I'm imagining that your perspective is not all that great.

Now, either sitting or standing, put a big grin on your face and stare up at the ceiling.

Keeping that big grin on your face, stare up at the ceiling and really grin. Your neck should be bent back and your eyes should be crinkled around the edges as that wide grin fills your face.

Engage every muscle in your face as you do this.

Don't stop smiling at the ceiling for at least 90 seconds.

While this probably feels a little crazy, keep going for the full 90 seconds. When the 90 seconds have passed, bring your head back to its normal position.

How do you feel now?

I can guarantee you that the one thing you don't feel is depressed.

While you may feel a little embarrassed, you probably also feel happy, relaxed, and maybe even a little more confident. You have changed your frame and you have a different perspective.

This is the power of your state.

Simply by transmuting your physiology, you transformed your frame and gave yourself a different, more powerful perceptive.

This new perspective also calmed your zombie mind, allowing your mammalian brain to take back control.

Now you, like Al, are no longer being held back by the problem. Instead, you're able to search for solutions that will allow you to move from where you are now, to where you want to be.

Your new perspective will help you achieve a new outcome. The outcome you really want to achieve.

Winning the Gold

Sometimes, to change your perspective all you need is a pick-me-up. While some people use chemicals to do this, your body can supply you with all the energy you need, simply by adopting the "winning the gold" posture.

The winning the gold posture is like the posture nearly all athletes assume after they win their respective event.

Google an Olympic champion and look at them right after they know that they've just won the gold medal.

No matter what event it is, after winning, they all adopt a similar posture. Jessica Tracy, a professor at the University of British Columbia, has named this posture "pride."

In the pride posture, the head tilts up, the chest is out, and the person has a slight smile on their face. Their hands are either firmly planted on their hips or raised high above their heads in clenched fists.[7]

The opposite of this posture is shame. In the shame posture, the losing person's shoulders slump, their chin goes down, and their chest narrows. This is a posture many people, such as Al, adopt when things aren't going well.

Tracy as well as David Matsumoto, a professor at San Francisco State University and a 7th degree black belt in judo who was also part of the Olympic Judo team, found that these postures were universal. This means they appear naturally in humans from all cultures.

The way they discovered this was by observing blind Paralympic athletes. What they observed was these athletes displayed the same postures as sighted athletes as they won or lost, even though most had been blind from birth. This would seem to imply that our bodies adopt these postures naturally.[8]

Let's say you, like Al, are having a bad day at the office.

You just had a meeting with your boss and you've been told that a report you've just spent the last eight hours working on isn't as complete as she hoped it would have been. She communicates her disappointment to you and gives you two hours to make some upgrades.

While she didn't chew you out, you leave the office feeling bad about yourself, even slightly depressed. Your shoulders are slumped and your eyes are boring holes into the ground.

At this point, you realize that if you don't change your attitude, you're going struggle mightily to complete the upgrades your boss wants in the time she allotted you.

Now your zombie mind starts to take over and you begin to slip into panic mode.

Here's what you need to do. Instead of letting your zombie mind take over and send you in a downward spiral, go somewhere that's a little private, bring your head up, stick your chest out, pump your fists in the air, and shout, "Yes!"

Do this a few times and then go back to work.

What you'll find is that you'll have a burst of energy to help you focus on what you need to focus on, in this case, the upgrades to the report that will give you the solution your boss is looking for.

Again, all you've done is change your frame. This change of frame has helped change your perspective about what's happening in the world around you.

With your new perspective, you can see new paths to the outcome you seek.

How to Focus Like a Trumpet Player

I played saxophone in elementary and junior high school. I loved creating music and entertaining people along with my fellow band members.

We had a very talented group of young band members, and as a result, we were a hot commodity on the elementary/junior high school band circuit.

One day at an event we were invited to play at, we watched as a very talented group of older (they had to be in their late teens or early 20s) musicians knocked the socks off the audience.

After they finished playing, I walked over to where one of the horn players was cleaning his trumpet. He looked at me and said something like, "What's up?"

I remember I smiled and said something like "Hi, not much" back, trying to remain cool. But then I blurted out something like, "You guys were awesome! What do I need to do to learn how to play like you guys?"

The trumpet player smiled and said, "You've got to focus on the balls of your feet."

I probably looked like I was completely lost (which I was) when he continued saying, "I learned this from an old guy a few years ago; he told me when you're playing, make sure to focus on the balls of your feet. It'll help you stay focused and more in control of your playing."

While this little technique did help me play my sax better, its real benefits didn't really hit me until years later when I was trying to pay attention in a college class. It was an early morning math class and I found that I had a hard time concentrating. As a result, I wasn't doing all that well.

While walking to class, I happened to walk by where a group of band members was practicing. As I listened to them play, the conversation with the trumpet player popped into my mind. As a result, I decided to try that technique as I listened in class.

What I found was that it worked amazingly well! Continually concentrating on the balls of my feet brought me back into the moment. It seemed like I was picking up everything the professor was explaining to us. So much so, that after leaving class that day I was actually able to explain a part of it to one of my classmates.

Since then, I've used this technique whenever I find my concentration drifting off, whether it be listening in a class or listening to a conversation. It has helped me stay focused and in the moment.

The great thing is that you can use this technique any time you need to hone in on what's going on.

Simply sit or stand up straight with your feet planted firmly on the ground and concentrate on the spots where the balls of your feet meet the ground.

Within moments, you'll find yourself more focused and in the moment, taking in everything you need to take in.

How to Create Superhuman Confidence

Your perspective can be devastating to your confidence. A lack of confidence will definitely affect your performance. Nowhere is this truer than when you're looking for a job.

Over the years, I've taught a lot of communications classes. One of the things often covered in these classes is how to prepare for an interview.

One of the biggest outcomes college students strive for is to be able to find a job in their field that allows them to live comfortably and pay off their student loans. While many of them are good with researching jobs and writing resumes and cover letters, a majority are anxious about talking with the interviewer.

For whatever reason, they just don't feel confident about their ability to go through the interview process.

As you probably already know, while a student needs to have a good grasp of the basic information needed for the position, what's even more important is for them to project an image of confidence about their ability to do the work, or at least learn to do the work, to the person or people they are interviewing with.

So, to help them with this, I teach them what I call the Superman or Superwoman (this is also called the Wonder Woman) technique.

What's really exciting is that science has found that this posture really works.

Recently, postures like the Superman or Superwoman have been studied in the lab by social scientists like Amy Cuddy, a professor at Harvard Business School. In her book *Presence, Bring Your Boldest Self to Your Biggest Challenges,*[14] Professor Cuddy discusses how practicing power poses, similar to the Superman or Superwoman pose, before an interview can give a big boost of confidence to the interviewee.

In one of her experiments, Professor Cuddy, along with Caroline Wilmuth, Dana Carney, and Andy Yap, measured how preparing for a job interview using power poses affected a person's evaluated performance and potential to be hired. What they found was, "Subjects who prepared for the job interview with high-power poses (versus low-power poses) performed significantly better and were significantly more likely to be 'hired' ..." [15]

It would seem to follow that these postures would also be extremely helpful for someone getting ready for a big meeting, a presentation, or even a big date.

Here's how Superman or Superwoman technique works.

Have you ever seen a Superman movie?

How about Superman or Supergirl on TV?

How does this powerful superhero stand?

They stand with their head up, shoulders back, and chest out. They probably have their hands on their hips.

---

[14] 2015, Little Brown and Company.
[15] 2015, Little Brown and Company. pp. 224-225

You can use this same posture to make yourself feel powerful and confident.

Right now, I'd like for you to imagine that you are Superman or Superwoman.

You could even imagine yourself as Wonder Woman or some other powerful superhero, just as long as you don't imagine yourself as Invisible Man or Invisible Woman.

Now adopt their powerful posture. Bring your shoulders back and your head up. Stick your chest out. Put your hands on your hips and a smile on your face.

Imagine how this superhero would walk and then take in a deep diaphragmic breath as you begin to walk slowly forward. Adopt your superhero's confident stride and imagine your cape billowing behind you.

I know this might feel funny, but stay with me for just another minute or so.

Now, imagine someone firing bullets at you and imagine the bullets bouncing off your chest as you continue to stride forward. Feel the confidence you have as you adopt the state of this superhero.

Feel how strong you are.

Now smile as you take in a deep, slow breath, and then let it out slowly. Now take in another deep, slow breath, and let it out. Now take in and let out another.

Let me ask you, "How do you feel right now?"

I imagine that you feel powerful and confident as well as ready to take on any challenge that comes your way.

The next time you have a big meeting with your boss, have to give a presentation, or go into an interview, use this technique. It will supply you with an abundance of confidence.

Now, I'm not suggesting that you walk into your meeting using this posture. But I am suggesting that you go someplace private, like the restroom, and practice this posture for a few minutes right before going to your meeting.

What you'll find is, just like the subjects in Professor Cuddy's experiments, you'll go into your meeting feeling powerful, super motivated, and confident.

You'll be a person other people like, listen to, and trust.

(I highly recommend that you write out the results of practicing these different postures. You can go to https://tinyurl.com/Mindful-Mastery-Journal to get your FREE interactive journal especially designed for this book.)

Chapter 34

The Dirty Eight-Letter
Word that Nobody Likes

"Health is the greatest possession. Contentment is the greatest treasure. Confidence is the greatest friend. Non-being is the greatest joy."

—Lao Tzu

While everything you've learned in the last chapter will help you take charge of your state, there is one final, dirty eight-letter word that I want to lay on you before we pull it all together.

Here's the word: **Exercise**.

Yes, I know that if you're like most people you absolutely detest this word and all it stands for. A comment I often hear about exercise is, "Why don't they just have a pill for that?"

First, as a full disclaimer, I enjoy exercise. While there are times that I would rather be doing anything else besides exercising, once I start my workout I find myself feeling fantastic. This is why I make myself exercise, even when I don't want to.

Over the years, my research has shown me that there are a number of scientific reasons behind this. Studies have found that, in addition to making your body fitter and leaner, exercise actually helps to sharpen your mind in a number quantifiable ways.

Here are a few examples:

In a 2003 article, Professor Phillip D. Tomporowski of the University of Georgia found that just 20 minutes of daily exercise aids a person's ability to process and remember information.[9]

Another 2004 article by Raffaella Molteni, Jun-Qi Zheng, Zhe Ying, Fernando Gómez-Pinilla, and Jeffery L. Twiss found that exercise helps improve brain plasticity through the stimulation of brain cell connections.

In their study, these researchers found that exercise increases growth factors in the brain that, in turn, helps the brain grow neuronal connections.[10]

Simply put, neuronal connections help your brain think and remember better.

Finally, a 2005 study by Astrid Bjørnebekk, Aleksander A. Mathé, and Stefan Brené at the University of Stockholm found that runners receive antidepressant-like effects that result in a drop in stress hormones.

This decrease allows for an increase in cell growth in the hippocampus, which is the part of the brain we humans use for learning and memory.[11]

The reason I bring this up is that there is no better medicine for your body and brain than a regular exercise program.

Making the decision to exercise for just 30 minutes a day is one of the best investments of time you can make. So, if you want to perform at a high level of peak performance, make exercise an integral part of your daily routine.

It will pay off both immediately with a stronger body and more energy, as well as in the long run with improved mental and physical health.

Now let's move on.

PART III

Application

Chapter 35

Dropping into the Zone

"Let the world know why you're here and do it with passion."

—Wayne Dyer

Imagine you are standing on the edge of the 876-foot-high New River Gorge Bridge in Fayetteville, West Virginia getting ready to BASE jump.

For those of you who aren't familiar, BASE jumping, also sometimes written as B.A.S.E. jumping, is parachuting from a fixed structure. "BASE" is an acronym standing for four categories of fixed objects from which you can jump. These are buildings, antennas, spans, and the earth.

You were in the area, so you decided you would jump today from the bridge.

You haven't jumped from here before so you bring along a local BASE jump instructor who checked your equipment one last time before you stepped to the edge. Taking deep belly breaths to calm your pounding heart, you take a quick glimpse down, then back to the instructor.

As you stand there, every second seems to be an eternity, but as soon as he gives you the thumbs up, and you lean forward, every thought slides from your mind.

You are focused and sure.

Your mind is completely on task. You have no doubt you can do this, as you hit the empty space.

Your chute opens perfectly and time seems to stand still as you gently slide to the ground below.

You feel at one with the universe.

Before you know it, you are on the ground looking up at the bridge, and you smile.

What you've just experienced is the state of flow.

Elements of Flow

Like the BASE jumper, when you're in the zone, you are **totally immersed** in what you are doing.

This intense focus will **skyrocket your productivity**.

The world goes on around you, but **you aren't distracted** by it.

This causes **time to lose its meaning**.

Your tasks become **deeply enjoyable** and you find yourself **stretching your abilities** to reach an even higher level of performance, **giving your life more meaning**.

These benefits are available to anyone who learns to harness the elements of flow.

Let's take a quick look at the different elements that make up the zone and how you can learn to recognize them.

Chapter 36

Complete Immersion in the Tasks at Hand

"Flow is important both because it makes the present instant more enjoyable, and because it builds the self-confidence that allows us to develop skills and make significant contributions to humankind."

—Dr. Mihaly Csikszentmihalyi

As Dr. Mihaly Csikszentmihalyi notes, in the flow state, nothing else seems to matter. You're so immersed in the task at hand that everything else fades far into the background. Nothing can disturb you.

This is such a pleasant experience, that this, by itself, is worth pursuing. When you experience being in the zone, you want to return to it over and over again. The zone is such an enjoyable place that it can turn even the most difficult jobs into pleasant experiences.

How do you focus your mind so much that you are totally immersed in what you do?

You can only drop into the zone when you're applying yourself to a worthy, challenging task. This is why you need to answer the universe question every morning.

What's Important?

Let's face it, you're going to have a difficult time getting into the zone if you're working on mundane things such as filing paperwork, writing emails, responding to notifications or making phone calls.

You need to set a challenging, worthy goal for yourself. A goal that will stretch you and require you to use your skills to the maximum.

Your goal is to use this intense focus to make significant contributions to humankind. In other words, to achieve something noble and worthy. Something that will make a dent in the world.

How can you do this?

You must be working on an important, significant task. A goal that lines up with the values you choose back in Chapter 24.

When choosing your task/goal, ask yourself these questions:

"What is my most important task right now?"

"What one thing would make everything else in my life easier?"

"What would make the most difference for me personally or professionally?"

"What will move the needle most for my business?"

In the book, *The One Thing: The Surprisingly Simple Truth Behind Extraordinary Results*,[16] Gary Keller recommends going small when choosing your goal.

In other words, choosing the ONE thing that will make the most difference when you accomplish it.

---

[16] 2013, Bard Press.

In the book Gary says, "'Going small' is ignoring all the things you could do and doing what you should do. It's recognizing that not all things matter equally and finding the things that matter most. It's a tighter way to connect what you do with what you want. It's realizing that extraordinary results are directly determined by how narrow you can make your focus."

If you want to enter flow state, avoid trying to do everything.

You need to focus on the ONE thing, a worthy goal that will stretch you and force you to fully engage with the task. Choose a task that will require your full attention.

By asking and answering the universe question we first talked about in Chapter 4 every morning, and then asking yourself the above questions, you will focus your mind in like a laser on finding and doing the most important tasks to do right now.

Now you are ready to drop into the zone.

Chapter 37

Skyrocketing Productivity

"Control of consciousness determines the quality of life."

—Dr. Mihaly Csikszentmihalyi

In the zone, your productivity skyrockets through the roof.

Why?

Because you're only focused on the task in front of you. One single task.

The ONE thing that will make a difference.

This is the opposite of multitasking, trying to do many things at one time. You're not simultaneously surfing Facebook, responding to emails, and texting your friends while trying to finish the project you're working on.

Instead of working on five different things at once, making very little progress on any of them, you are totally immersed in what you are doing. This keeps you zoned in and focused on what you've decided is the most important task to do at this moment.

This single focus expands your abilities, allowing you to pull in more of your skills and strengths. Now you can dedicate every ounce of your energy toward achieving that single goal.

As you focus directly on that ONE thing, you make the maximum progress possible. This allows you to achieve more in one hour in the zone than you do in the many hours outside of it.

How to Skyrocket Your Productivity

"The secret of passion is purpose."

—Robin Sharma

When seeking to enter flow state, it's important to be very specific about exactly what you're trying to accomplish during a specific period of time.

You must set a time limit for yourself and then choose what you're going to accomplish during that time.

Setting boundaries forces you to concentrate very quickly. This prevents you from wasting your most precious resource—time.

For example, let's say that you want to complete the first section of a report that you've been putting off because you know it will be hard.

Give yourself one hour (or whatever is reasonable) to complete the first section. During that hour, focus intensely on completing your goal. Give all your attention to completing the sales report and avoid letting anything distract you.

While you're working on the report avoid email, text messages, and apps like Skype or Slack.

Commit yourself fully to completing the first section of the sales report.

Now that you've made your commitment, don't let anything keep you from achieving your goal.

Do one thing and only one thing during your period of intense concentration.

Pomodoro Method

You may want to consider using the Pomodoro method to help you drop into the zone.

(I highly recommended that you record the results your receive using the Pomodoro Method in your journal. You can go to https://tinyurl.com/Mindful-Mastery-Journal to get your FREE interactive journal especially designed for this book.)

Here's how the Pomodoro method works:

Set a timer for 25 minutes and work intensely (no distractions!) for that 25-minute period.

After 25 minutes, take a 5-minute break to let your brain rest (remember the breather we talked about in Chapter 32?)

During these five minutes, you can do whatever you want.

Go back to work for another 25-minute session. Follow this session with another 5-minute break.

After you go through four 25-minute sessions, take a 15-minute break.

Now, repeat the process

By using the Pomodoro method, you force yourself to focus intensely for 25 minutes with no distractions.

This allows you (even forces you) to drop into the zone much more easily.

Don't allow yourself the option of messing around on your phone or checking email. You must ruthlessly focus on accomplishing your goal.

This is how you drop into the zone and skyrocket your productivity.

Give Yourself Enough Time

It's important to note that you need to give yourself enough time to drop into the zone. For example, if you have to pick up your kids from school in 15 minutes, this is not a sufficient amount of time to immerse yourself in your task.

Ideally, give yourself at least 25-30 minutes. Give yourself more time if possible.

Your brain won't immediately snap into flow state the second you start. It just doesn't work that way.

It takes some time for you to focus and tune out distractions. This is why using the Pomodoro method is so useful.

Chapter 38

Block Out All Distractions

"Concentrate all your thoughts upon the work at hand. The sun's rays do not burn until brought to a focus. When you concentrate all your thoughts on the work at hand, you can achieve extraordinary things."

—Alexander Graham Bell

One day a young girl was having trouble paying attention to her studies. She was whispering to her neighbors, looking out the window and glancing at the door.

Her teacher asked her, "What's going on?"

"Oh, this stuff is too boring. I don't know why I should even pay attention to it!" the little girl answered.

Grabbing a newspaper from her desk, the teacher reached into one of her desk drawers, pulled something from it and put it in her pocket. "Let's go outside," she told the class.

It was a clear, bright sunny day. The teacher walked to the middle of the playground and crumpled a few pages of the newspaper into a ball.

Setting the newspaper ball on the ground, she reached into her pocket. She pulled out a magnifying glass.

She moved the magnifying glass from side to side over the crumpled pages.

Nothing happened.

Then she held the magnifying glass still. The sun's rays focused in on a spot and in a short while, the paper burst into flames.

The teacher smiled and looked at the little girl. Then she said, "Your mind is like this magnifying glass."

The little girl gave her teacher a puzzled look.

Her teacher continued, "When the magnifying glass was moving, even though the sun rays were moving through it, nothing happened, right?"

The little girl nodded.

"But when you hold it still you can harness the power of the sun and multiply its power through the lens. That's how we started the fire."

"Focusing also works with the power of your thoughts. When you pay attention to what you are doing you can ignite your mind and accomplish a lot!"

Focused Power

While right now, the thought of not experiencing any distractions may seem impossible to you, when you truly enter the zone, your brain shuts out everything except what you're working on.

This is how you magnify the power within you.

Now, to be clear, there are some steps you'll need to take to minimize distractions, especially in the beginning.

We'll get into that in a bit.

Just for a moment, imagine what it would be like being able to work distraction free. Imagine being able to shut out, at will, all notifications, buzzes, dings, pings, alerts and every other distracting noise.

Imagine being so in the moment that nothing else seems to matter. How focused would you be?

Imagine how much more you could accomplish if you were able to focus completely on achieving the one thing that matters most to you in that moment. This is what happens when you are able to work in the zone.

Getting Rid of the Interference

"You'll never achieve flow if you're distracted. Your brain just can't handle it. Certainly, there are circumstances in which distractions are unavoidable. But much of the time, you can work to minimize or eliminate distractions."

—Ransom Patterson

As Ransom Patterson points out, blocking out distractions is absolutely essential to be able to drop into the zone. You can't enter the flow state when you can't concentrate.

Here's how to eliminate distractions.

If you're hungry, get something to eat. Now you won't be thinking about how hungry you are.

This next one is the easiest, yet few people do it. Put your phone on silent or even airplane mode.

Close your email. Also, close all your chat programs like Slack and Skype.

Close all unnecessary tabs on your browser, especially distracting ones such as social media or your news feed.

Close your door. If you can't close your door, put on headphones and listen to background music that helps you concentrate.

No More Interruptions

If you do all the steps above and still find yourself getting distracted, you may need to take even more extreme measures.

Here's a few suggestions on how to completely get rid of all the interruptions.

Actively block social media sites using site-blocking software. Apps like RescueTim can do this for you. These apps won't allow you to use specified sites (like Facebook) once you activate them. When you try to go to one of the blocked sites, it simply won't work. If you are someone who is distracted by sites like Facebook or Reddit, this will be a huge help.

Find focus music you enjoy. For example, Brain.fm can be very helpful for blocking out background noise.

They have a variety of different types of music and sound, all scientifically designed to help you focus more. This kind of music can work wonders, especially if you find yourself distracted by noise.

What you want to do is block anything that might distract you from the task at hand.

You can't slip into the zone if you aren't giving 100% of your attention to the task you have chosen. Anything cutting into your focus needs to be completely eliminated.

Do everything in your power to remove every distraction.

Chapter 39

You Totally Lose Track of Time

"Everyone has the gift of time, but few utilize."

—M.K. Soni

Can you remember doing something and time just seemed to stand still?

Maybe it was when you were a child, playing with friends.

Maybe it was when you were working on something you love.

Maybe it was spending time with a close friend or loved one.

Those were times when you were in the zone. In the zone, time seems to stand still.

Why?

Because you're completely immersed in what you're doing.

You look up and, instead of minutes, you find you've spent hours doing whatever it was you were doing.

This is the biggest reason you are so much more productive in flow state.

By dedicating your total consciousness to what you are doing, you can get significantly more done.

Increased Enjoyment of the Task

Many people spend a lot of time in the past. The problem with the past is it is a place filled with regret.

Other people spend a lot of time in the future. The problem with the future is it is a place filled with imaginary worries.

But the past and future are only illusions. You can only work on things now, in the present. The present is the only place where you can accomplish anything.

Spending time in the past or future just fills you with regrets and makes you feel worried and anxious. On the other hand, when you're in the zone, you're living in the here and now instead of thinking about the past or future.

In the zone, you're not thinking about the problems in your life. You're not worried about that report that you need to file. You're not preoccupied with that meeting that you still haven't prepared for.

This is because these things are not even on your radar.

The only thing you're thinking about right now is what you're working on. Your focus is in a single spot, instead of scattered about by a thousand different thoughts and worries.

In the zone all your worries, fears, and struggles take a temporary back seat. Your brain simply doesn't have the time or energy to think about them.

Your brain doesn't have the mental capacity to focus fully on your work and also entertain these worries. The result is a hyper-productive bliss.

Getting Time to Stand Still

If you find you aren't able to slip into the zone, one of the easiest ways to focus your mind in the present is to practice the belly breathing technique you learned in Chapter 21.

A simple way to regain your focus is to use the following mindfulness technique.

Go to as quiet a place as possible.

As you breathe in, think to yourself, "I am here and now."

As you breathe out, imagine your thoughts as soft-colored wispy, floating things that you are letting go as you breathe out.

Not only will this bring you into the here and now, it will oxygenate your blood and give you the energy you need to focus completely on what you are doing.

Chapter 40

You're Stretching Your Abilities

"Contrary to what we usually believe, moments like these, the best moments in our lives, are not the passive, receptive, relaxing times....The best moments usually occur when a person's body or mind is stretched to its limits in a voluntary effort to accomplish something difficult and worthwhile."

—Dr. Csikszentmihalyi

group of frogs was traveling through woods and two accidentally fell onto the edge of a deep pit filled with rocks at the bottom. The frogs above saw how steep the edge of the pit was and figured there was no hope for their two comrades to escape.

Both frogs struggled to get out of the pit many times but failed again and again.

The other frogs could hear them panting and groaning from their effort. They could tell from their groans they were in great pain.

Trying to prevent them from experiencing any more useless pain, the frogs above shouted to them to give up. They could see that escaping was impossible.

After a while, one frog took their advice and gave up, falling swiftly to his death on the rocks below. However, the other frog kept trying and, after much effort, finally pushed his way to the top.

Amazed, the other frogs asked him, "Didn't you hear us? We were telling you to give up!"

Looking at his companions with dismay, the frog explained that he was deaf and thought other frogs were encouraging him to get out.

That's why he was able to escape.

It's Time to Stretch

To escape the everyday world and enter the flow state, you, like the frog, need to stop listening to those who tell you that what you're trying to do is too hard.

It's only too hard for those who won't give it their all. Those who won't stretch their abilities.

To get into a flow state you must be tackling worthy, challenging goals. You need to be using the gifts, talents and strengths you've been given to the utmost of your ability.

As we've discussed, you can't get into flow state when you're working on mundane, tedious tasks. All that will happen is your brain will wander and you'll easily get distracted.

To enter the zone you must work on a task that requires you to stretch yourself, sometimes physically as well as mentally. This allows you to tap into your gifts and abilities as you fully apply your mental energy to what's in front of you.

Doing What's Most Important

In Chapter 4, you began developing your habit of writing down what you would do with your life if all the forces in the universe were to suddenly come together for you. In other words, if you won the lottery, how would you live your life?

In Chapter 17, we talked about working backwards, or outcome-based thinking, to create your goals. This is deciding on what outcome you desire and then figuring out what it takes to make it happen.

In Chapter 24, you did an exercise that examined what you value and then listed your top five values in order of importance – to you. The values you choose help guide you in deciding where you put your energy.

These exercises are to get you going in the right direction.

Now it's time to get your mind focused on goals that will drop you into the zone.

How do you to this?

You do this by asking why.

Why – Why – Why – Why – Why?

Your goals need to be so compelling that they drive you to work on them. They need to be irresistible.

To create irresistible goals you're going to use what's known as the 5-Why process. This 5-Why process comes from a technique that's used in the Analyze phase of the Six Sigma DMAIC (Define, Measure, Analyze, Improve, Control) methodology.

Why?

When you ask the question, "Why?" you begin to remove illusions that surround a problem and get to its root cause.

We're going to use why here to help you make sure that your why is really **THE** why behind your lifetime outcome.

Think about it like this. Children are always asking why.

Let's say, for example, you put on a suit and are getting ready for a big meeting at work.

Your daughter comes into the room and asks, "(Daddy/ Mommy), why are you wearing that?"

You answer, "Because I have a big meeting at work."

Then she asks, "Why do you have to wear a suit for a big meeting?"

"Because people expect me to wear a suit at a big meeting."

Looking puzzled she says, "Why do they expect you to wear a suit?"

"Because everyone else wears a suit."

As her brow furrows and she asks, "So why does everyone wear a suit?"

"I guess it's because it's kind of like our business uniform, kind of like your school uniform"

Looking extremely puzzled, she queries, "Why do you have to wear a uniform at work?"

"I guess it's because we all feel more comfortable with each other. Feeling comfortable with each other helps us trust each other. When we trust each other, we can work more easily with each other."

Ah, out of the mouth of a child!

Notice that the answer here went from the very superficial answer of, "Because I have a big meeting at work" to the very real answer of, "When we trust each other, we can work more easily with each other."

By digging down to the fifth why the businessperson was able to uncover her source.

While your kids can drive you crazy asking so many why questions, using this process, called the 5-Why process, can get to the very core of why you decide to do what you do.

This is the beauty of this process. The 5-Why process gives you the very essence of your source.

Let's go through this process again. This time we'll pretend that you have set a goal to make $250,000 this year.

Ask yourself, "Why do I want to make $250,000 this year?"

You answer might be, "Because this would give me enough money that I could save to start my own business."

Again, you ask, "Why do I want to start my own business?"

You answer: "Because I would be able to concentrate on doing the things I want to do."

Another why: "Why do I want to concentrate on doing the things I want to do?"

Another answer: "Because those are the things I feel I'm really good at."

You ask again, "Why do I want to do the things I feel I'm really good at?"

Your answer is, "Because when I'm doing what I'm good at I feel like I'm not even working. I'm totally in the zone."

Your final question is "Why do I want to feel like I'm totally in the zone?"

Your deep reason uncovers itself when you respond by saying, "Because then it's not work, it's fun. It's here where I feel free."

The 5-Why process uncovered that the root cause for making $250,000 isn't to save enough money that you can start your own business. Your real why, the source of this compulsion, is the feeling of freedom you can achieve from working for yourself.

Now it's time to put the 5-Why process to work for you. Take at least 20 minutes to go through the 5-Why process with your personal and professional lifetime outcomes. Write down each why answer in your journal.

(To record your experience of the 5-Why process, you can go to https://tinyurl.com/Mindful-Mastery-Journal to get your FREE interactive journal especially designed for this book.)

Once you've done this, you're ready stretch yourself.

Chapter 41

Find What Stretches You

"While on top of Everest, I looked across the valley towards the great peak Makalu and mentally worked out a route about how it could be climbed. It showed me that even though I was standing on top of the world, it wasn't the end of everything. I was still looking beyond to other interesting challenges."

—Sir Edmund Hillary

n January 1969, Bruce Lee penned a letter to himself. It read as follows:

"My Definite Chief Aim

I, Bruce Lee, will be the first highest paid Oriental super star in the United States. In return, I will give the most exciting performances and render the best of quality in the capacity of an actor. Starting 1970 I will achieve world fame and from then onward till the end of 1980 I will have in my possession $10,000,000. I will live the way I please and achieve inner harmony and happiness."

Bruce Lee

After penning this letter to himself, Bruce Lee went on to rise to stardom in China by landing the starring role in *The Big Boss*, a martial arts movie classic. Before his untimely passing in 1973, he also rose to stardom in the United States.

The rest is history.

Bruce Lee figured out what his deep why was and then stretched himself to reach the goals that fulfilled his why. As a result, Bruce was able to access flow state at will.

So can you.

Take the time to find your why. This will drive you to set goals that use all your gifts, strengths, and abilities you have to achieve them.

Goals that will stretch you. Goals that drive you. Goals that keep you going in the face of adversity.

Doing this will so focus you on what you're doing, that you, like Bruce Lee, will be able to achieve something truly worthwhile with your life.

What are you waiting for?

Chapter 42

Your Life has More Meaning

"Ability is what you're capable of doing. Motivation determines what you do. Attitude determines how well you do it."

—Lou Holtz

An old man lived in a village where everyone had grown tired of him. He constantly complained, never had a good word to say to anyone, and was always in a bad mood.

As he grew older, his words became viler and more venomous. As you would expect, people did their best to avoid him. Anyone who encountered him left with a feeling of dread and unhappiness.

The day he turned eighty, everything changed.

It was incredible.

The whole village was saying, "The old man is happy today. He doesn't complain about anything. He smiles at everyone. He looks so different!"

Gathering around the old man, someone finally asked, "What happened to you?"

The old man replied, "I've been chasing happiness for eighty years and I could never catch it. Today I decided to relax and quit chasing it."

The villagers quietly looked at the old man, expectedly waiting for more information.

Smiling the old man finally said, "Instead I decided to live without happiness and just enjoy life. This is why I'm happy now.'"

A Change in Attitude

"Your attitude, not your aptitude, will determine your altitude."

—Zig Ziglar

He is 100% correct.

Just as the story about the old man illustrates, your attitude affects you and everyone around you. If you have a negative outlook on life, like the old man had for most of his life, you will remain stuck and people will avoid you.

On the other hand, if you stop chasing the kind of happiness that comes from the outside world and just decide to enjoy life, like the old man, you can begin to have the kind of life that brings your happiness and pulls you into the zone.

As you've already discovered, the zone is a place where you must work on something that requires you to stretch yourself. You must be able to give yourself fully to it or you will continue to run into roadblocks and barriers.

If you spend your time on the mundane, social media, email, the news, and office gossip, you will never have time to reach flow state. To access the zone, you must be dedicating a significant portion of your time to tasks that are meaningful to your life's journey.

Doing this will allow you to experience the kind of motivation that will get you out of bed every morning, looking forward to your new day.

You will experience true happiness as you give yourself fully to something that actually matters to you. Something that brings you joy and moves the needle forward for you personally, professionally or spiritually.

This will help you to accomplish even more and add even more joy, which will lead to a much more meaningful life.

This is why once you experience dropping into the zone, you'll want to repeat it over and over and over again.

The great news is, since you've come this far, you already know how to do all this.

Now, let's take a look at how convergence can help you drop into the zone.

Chapter 43

Converging into the Zone

"Opportunities to find deeper powers within ourselves come when life seems most challenging."

—Joseph Campbell

et's be honest. No matter how far we've gone and how much we have achieved, we all get stuck at times. We reach a certain point in our lives where it seems that no matter how much effort we put in, the next level is just out of our reach.

When we look at the people who have already achieved the level we struggle to reach, we wonder, "How did they get there? Did they know somebody? Were they lucky? Do they have some kind of secret mojo that propelled them to where they are today?"

The answer would almost always be, "Of course not!"

The reason they were able to reach that level was because they got it all together; they were able to converge their why, their beliefs, and their state in such a powerful manner that they could overcome or bypass the barriers that they encountered along their path.

This enabled them to drop easily into the zone, whenever and wherever they wanted. This is how convergence works.

For example, as you may already know, one of the things many people relate martial arts to, and especially black belts, is breaking boards.

Here's what I've learned after over four decades practicing martial arts, breaking who-knows-how-many boards, and training many, many other people to break boards.

Are you ready for it?

It's not about the board.

Breaking a board, how you break the board, and the number of boards you break have nothing to do with the board at all.

It's about YOU.

It's about the mindset of the person breaking the board.

The difference between a board breaker and a non-board breaker is they have learned how to pull it all together. They mastered breaking the board in their mind before attempting to break it.

They know exactly why they're breaking the board.

They believe they can break the board.

And they know how to put their body into the right state to break the board.

This allows them to drop into the zone and break the board easily.

No fuss, no muss.

Ann vs. Andrew

Many years ago, I taught a couple of martial arts students that I still vividly remember to this day. Let's call them Ann and Andrew.

Andrew was six-feet-two-inches tall and weighed about one hundred and ninety-five pounds. He was a former college athlete and, while he had never become an elite athlete, he was very talented athletically. He was also someone who had relied all his life on his innate ability and strength to do well in the sports he had competed in.

On the other hand, Ann was a petite mother of two young children, both of whom had been taking classes for a couple of weeks before she started taking classes. She worked in administration in a local business and, along with her husband, raised her kids.

One thing for sure about Ann was no one would confuse her with being extremely athletic.

One day, as she was picking her children up from their class, she saw some of the adult students practicing. She thought, "I can do this" and began taking lessons.

She started taking her classes around the same time as Andrew. They both worked out together in the same class and had been promoted to orange belt at the same time.

Now, back to board breaking.

Board breaking is a part of the green belt test. In order to advance from orange belt to green belt, a student is required to break a board. Depending on their age, they have a choice to break it with a kick (their foot) a hand technique or their elbow.

At their orange belt test, their friend Tom, who was a few months ahead of them, had failed to break his board. He had decided to punch the board but didn't succeed. This meant he would have to re-take his test for green belt.

As a result, many of the orange belts were very concerned about being able to break a board for their upcoming test. Hearing a couple of them worriedly discussing this one day, I gathered the orange belts together.

"We're going to have a board breaking class for anybody who wants to come," I told them.

Immediately, all the orange belts signed up, including Ann and Andrew.

They were required to bring their notebooks to the first board breaking class. As they sat there, I said, "Okay, before we start physical practice, we will need to do some mental exercises."

I smiled and continued, "Write these two questions in your notebook and bring your answers back with you to the next class."

"Are you ready?"

Looking expectedly, they all nodded.

Then I had them write down the universe question and the lottery question.

After they finished writing we talked about the questions for a few minutes, then I told them, "That's it!"

All the orange belts got up and headed for the changing room, except one: Andrew.

Striding over to me, he asked, "You're not going to have us break boards today?"

"No," I replied, "We have nine weeks until the exam. The two questions we talked about tonight will help you get you started."

Almost scowling, Andrew gave me a sloppy bow and left for the dressing room.

The next week Andrew didn't show up to the board breaking class, but Ann was there with the rest of the orange belts.

"Did everyone do their assignment?" I asked.

Everyone nodded.

"Great! Does anyone want to share?"

A few students raised their hands. One by one they shared what they had written. Then Ann took her turn.

She said, "If all the forces in the universe would come together for me, I would continue working as hard as I can to be the best mom I can be."

All the students nodded their approval.

"Excellent," I told the class. Now, let's work on this week's assignment.

Together they learned about outcome-based thinking as well as long-term goals, milestones and stepping-stones. They also learned about staying positive, focusing their goals on themselves, staying in the right context and, of course, doing no harm.

After discussing the assignment for a while, I finally said, "Okay, that's it for today's class."

One of the students raised his hand.

"Yes?" I asked.

The student looked around the room and asked, "When are we going to work on breaking boards?"

I smiled and said, "Have a little patience. You'll get to break a board soon enough."

"Thank you," the student said, still looking a little puzzled.

Understanding his confusion, I told the class, "You have to be able to break the board in your mind before you can break it here in the world. If you are patient, you will find that you will be able to break any board."

"Yes sir!" he shouted in reply. All the students looked slightly more comfortable as they left.

At the next week's class, I had them all sit down and practice the 60-second exercise to keep track of their random thoughts. After we finished that, I had them practice their mindful breathing for five minutes.

The final thing we did at the class was set their intention.

"Write these three questions in your notebooks," I told them.

"What do I want to do?"

Then I said, "How many of you want to break a board at your green belt test?"

All of them raised their hands.

"Good! Write that down."

Now write this question down, "How will I measure it?"

"That's easy," one of them replied, "Does the board break or not?"

All the students laughed as I said, "Exactly!"

The third question is, "What will I give to get what I want?"

Another student hesitantly raised her hand and said, "Coming to this class?"

Everyone nodded in agreement.

"You all are right on track," I told them. "See you next week!"

The students left a little more excited than when they arrived that night, armed with a better understanding of what they were doing.

The next week the first thing we practiced was mindful breathing. After that I told them, "This week you're going to have two assignments. The first thing is to keep track of what your zombie voice is telling you."

After explaining what their zombie voice was and how to keep track of it, I handed out a list of values and said, "Your second assignment is to go through this list and choose your top five values."

Then I explained how they should use the list.

The whole class was sitting anxiously the next week when the class started. One asked, "I kept track of the zombie voice last week. It seems like I'm telling myself a lot of negative things."

Smiling, I said, "That's normal. We all tell ourselves a lot of negative things. That's why I had you do the exercise."

"So, what can we do about it?" he asked.

"You can use the 5-R process."

Then I explained the 5-R process to them and told them to work on the process the following week. Afterwards I had them practice mindful breathing again.

At the end of the class I told them, "Next week when you come, you will know how to break a board."

All the students smiled and talked excitedly among themselves as they left. One said she couldn't wait for the next week's lesson.

The next week, I told them the story about the old man at Pinky's Tattoo parlor. Then I explained that in order to overcome the inner zombie you had to acknowledge it and then shift it by creating an affirmation and then saying the affirmation aloud.

This is when Ann raised her hand. "I appreciate all you've been doing to help us but I don't think I can do this. Maybe board breaking just isn't for me."

Thinking back to my black belt test so many years before, I could really empathize with how Ann felt, so I asked her, "Why do you want break the board?"

She answered, "I'm not so sure I want to break the board!"

"Okay, if you wanted to break the board, why would you want to break the board?"

She thought for a moment and answered, "To pass my test,"

Then I asked, "Why do you want to pass your test?"

Ann answered, "So I can earn my green belt."

So why do you want to earn your green belt?"

"It's the next step to black belt."

"So why do you want to earn a black belt?"

"Because it'll make me feel good."

"Why will it make you feel good?"

"Because I'll be a good example for my kids."

"So, you're taking your test to be a good example for your kids, right?"

"Yes!"

Helping her through the 5-Why processes Ann was able to get to her root why. You could see the determination in her eyes as we finished.

After explaining the 5-Why process to the class, I told them, "Go home and go through this process on your own. You're almost ready to break your boards!"

The students were talking excitedly among themselves the next week as the class started. I had some of them share what they discovered by going through the 5-Why process.

Then, since I hadn't gone through it the previous week, we talked about the 5-R process. Many of the students shared what they had found going through the process when Ann again, raised here hand.

"I've been trying to go through this process but I keep getting stuck."

"What do you mean by stuck, Ann?" I asked her.

"I keep trying to tell myself I can break the board, but I don't really think I can," she said, her face tightening.

"Alright, let's watch a video for a few minutes."

I brought out a video of the last test showing all the people who had successfully broken their board. This included kids as young as seven.

Then I asked Ann, "Do you believe it's possible to break a board?"

"Yes," Ann agreed weakly, "it's possible."

"Do you believe you can break the board?"

Her lips pursed as she weakly murmured, "Yes."

I looked at her and said, "You don't seem very confident. Do you really believe you can break the board?"

Ann shook her head, saying "I-I don't know."

"Ann," I said, "You have a voice telling you something. Close your eyes and listen. What is that voice telling you?"

Ann closed her eyes and thought for a moment before responding. Finally, she said, "It's telling me it's too hard. It's telling me I won't break the board."

"Whose voice is it? Close your eyes again and think about it."

Ann looked puzzled for a moment and then closed her eyes. Finally, she said, "It sounds like my mother's voice."

"Okay, where is that voice? Is it inside you or outside you?"

"It's inside me."

"Where?"

"In my head, right by my left ear."

"Is it loud or soft?"

"She's whispering it to me."

Then I asked Ann, "What happens if you make that voice into a Mickey Mouse voice?"

Ann giggled and, after concentrating for a moment, she smiled.

"Now, what happens if you move that voice behind you about five feet?"

Ann replied, "It's hard to hear."

"Okay, push it 25 feet behind you. How does it seem now?"

"I can hardly hear it. I don't even notice it."

"Great," I said, "Now say to yourself, 'I am focused and powerful. No board can stop me!'"

Ann repeated, "I am focused and powerful. No board can stop me!"

I had her repeat the phrase for about a minute, then I said, "This time, after you finish saying your new phase, pump your arms into the air and say 'YES!'"

As the class watched, Ann and I practiced doing this a couple more times. Everyone could see how confident she looked when she finished.

"This is how you use the 5-R process," I told them.

Then I worked with each of them one at a time for the next half-hour. Afterwards I told them, "Next week you're going to learn how to use your body to break a board."

After pausing for a few seconds I asked, "Is everyone ready for this?"

"Yes sir!" they all shouted. They all seemed to be a lot more confident as they left class that night.

The class was quiet the next time as we started.

"Everyone looks so serious," I remarked.

A few of the students chuckled.

"Today you're going to learn how to get your body ready to break a board. The first part is easy. You've been practicing it since our second week together."

Raising his hand, a student asked, "What have we been practicing sir?"

"Mindful breathing," I answered.

Then I explained how mindful breathing activates the rest and digest response.

"This is how you keep your lizard mind from hijacking your mind and then missing hitting the board where you want."

Leaning forward, the students waited for me to continue.

"Now I want to teach you two other techniques for preparing your body. The first is something I learned from a trumpet player."

I explained to the students how focusing on the balls of their feet kept them in the moment. All of them stood and practiced for a few minutes.

Afterwards I said, "I have one more technique for you this week."

This is when I taught them the Superman/woman–Wonder Woman technique. I had all of them work on it with me.

Then I said, "Practice this for the next fifteen minutes."

A couple of minutes later, Ann came over and said, "I'm still not sure I can break the board."

"Take a deep breath,'" I told her.

As she took her deep breath, I told her to smile.

As she smiled, I told her, "Bring your head up, push out your chest and put your hands on your hips."

Ann followed my instructions, and then I said, "Now, imagine you are going up to the board you are going to break."

You could see the confidence rising in Ann as she stood there.

"Now walk, pretending you are walking up to the board you are about to break."

Ann took about a dozen steps, then I said, "Are you are ready?"

"YES!" she replied.

Then I asked her, "Do you believe you can break the board?"

"YES!" she shouted.

"Great!"

This took about five minutes. It was easy to see that Ann was in the zone.

The students who had been watching went back to practicing.

At the end of the class I told them, "You now have learned almost everything you need to know to break a board. Next week, you're going to put all of this knowledge to use."

A student raised her hand, "Does this mean we're going to break boards next week?'

"Most definitely," I answered.

With that I dismissed the class.

Chapter 44

Astronaut's Success Secret

"Great performers - in sports, the arts, business, or whatever field - have undertaken massive amounts of training. And when that training is complete... they train some more, and harder than they expect to perform. Why? Training builds confidence and ensures peak performance."

—Brandon Webb

efore we go back to board breaking, I want to ask you a question: "How do humans think?"

When asked this question, most people reply that we think in thoughts. You know, kind of like those thought bubbles you see in comic books.

But research suggests we use all of our senses—sight, sound, touch, hearing, smell and taste—when we think.

In NLP or Neuro-Linguistic Programming, which we talked about earlier, we use the power of the senses to boost the intensity of visualization even further.

Psychologists call this "embodied cognition," which is the idea that all our thoughts relate back to our physical experience.

When someone says something to you, or when you think something, the way you give it meaning is by using all your senses to experience it.

For example, think about walking through the snow. What is your brain telling you?

If you've walked through snow, you probably visualize the color white, feel cool air on your skin and hear the crunching sound the snow makes as you walk over it. Maybe you smell the freshness of the snow.

This is using all your senses to experience the concept you know as snow.

Here's something else you need to know about visualization. Research shows that the same areas of your brain light up in an MRI while you are imagining something as when you are actually doing it.

For example, imagine the smell and taste of chocolate chip cookies. Close your eyes.

Smell their deliciousness. Imagine taking that first bite as the chocolate chips melt in your mouth.

Right now, as far as your brain and body are concerned, you are eating a chocolate chip cookie!

Visualization can be used to persuade or convince you and, it's not a "trick."

It is using your mind to bring back certain images that you can attach to certain emotions. Just like in a movie.

This is the true beauty of visualization. You can use visualization to see your goals as if they were already accomplished.

But to maximize the power of visualization, you need to go one step further. You need to use visualization the way astronauts and world-class athletes use it.

You need to turn visualization into simulation.

Simulation is the process of visualizing your goals, then figuring out, and then simulating, the process of how you'll actually achieve them.

Here's how simulation works.

There was an experiment done with two groups of college students. One group visualized getting the grade they desired. The second group simulated the process they needed to undertake to get the grade they desired.

In other words, they would simulate studying a certain number of hours a day. They would simulate meeting with a study group. They would simulate getting enough sleep the night before an exam.

Then they would visualize themselves taking the exam and getting the grade they desired.

They also simulated problems they might encounter. People inviting them to parties. Study partners that flaked out.

Here's the bottom line.

The group that simulated received, on average, a whole letter grade higher than the group that had only visualized.

Simulation works better than simple visualization.

This is because simulation makes you think through the processes and the problems you'll encounter. This way, when a problem does come up, you will much more likely be able to handle it.

Simulated Board Breaking

At the next class, the students all sat attentively as I began the class. "Alright," I said, "Today you're going to break a board, in your mind."

One of the student's raised his hand and said, "We're not going to break a board?"

"Yes, you are," I replied. "In your mind." Then I explained, "What you just learned in this chapter, that experiencing something in your mind has the same effect on your mind as actually doing it."

I told them, "Sit comfortably, with your back straight, but relaxed."

"You're relaxed and alert as you focus on your breathing."

I had them concentrate on their breathing, having them breathe mindfully.

After a couple of minutes, I told them, "Imagine, right now, the day of your belt test. Imagine your goal, to earn your green belt."

"Now, in your mind, picture, imagine the real reason you want to pass your test."

I could see some of the students nodding.

"Now see yourself as you've done all the work to reach where you are today."

I waited quietly as they remembered all the work they had completed to reach this place in their training.

Then I said, "Take a deep breath, and stand up, keeping your eyes closed."

They all stood up.

"Now concentrate on the balls of your feet."

The students shuffled as they fixed their attention on the balls of their feet.

"Now, open your eyes and imagine the board is about ten feet in front of you. Use your Superman/woman posture to walk over to the board."

The students moved forward.

"Take a deep breath and let it out slowly."

The students took their breaths.

"Okay, visualize breaking the board. Move your hand or foot or elbow exactly as you would to break the board."

All the students focused, and then, letting out a loud Kiap, they performed their techniques.

"Did you break the board?" I asked.

"Yes sir!" they all shouted.

"That's it for this lesson, and for the class," I said. "I look forward to seeing you break your boards next Saturday!"

Back to Ann and Andrew

The next Saturday the orange belts were called up, one by one, to break their boards. As Ann approached her board, looking a little like Wonder Woman, she took a deep breath, letting it out slowly.

She moved her feet slightly as she prepared to break her board with a palm strike.

She breathed in, and then let it out slowly. Then with a loud Kiap she drove her palm at the board.

Can you imagine what happened?

You're right!

Ann snapped the board in two as easily as a hot knife slices through butter.

On the other hand, Andrew approached the board. As the assistants held it tightly, Andrew drew his hand back and punched the board as hard as he could.

There was a resounding thud as Andrew failed to break the board. In fact, he hit the board so poorly that he nearly broke his hand. His hand was sprained so badly that he had to carry it around in a sling for the following two weeks.

Not only was that embarrassing, it was painful.

When he finally returned to class, I asked him why he hadn't continued attending the workshop. He told me he thought he'd be able to muscle through it, just like everything else he'd done in life.

Let me ask you a question: what was the real difference between Ann and Andrew?

Ann took the time to learn how to converge the power of her mind, body, and spirit. This allowed her to place her energy and focus exactly where it needed to be, so she could drop into the zone and do exactly what she had set out to do—break the board.

Here's what you need to remember.

Breaking boards is exactly the same as getting your breakthrough in life. Your breakthrough will come when you align your mind, body, and spirit on what you want, at the right time, and at the right place, so you can drop into the zone and do exactly what you set out to do, whatever that may be.

Conclusion

"A coward gets scared and quits, the hero gets scared but still goes on. Same stimuli, different response. Be the hero."

—Wil Dieck

After going through this book, let me ask, "What is it you want to be?"

I hope that you've got a lot better handle on this idea now than when you started down this path with me.

Here's what I want to be.

Ever since I started taking judo classes in junior high school, I wanted to be a black belt. This changed to wanting to be a martial arts teacher after I achieved that goal, which reminds me of another story.

One day, as I was sitting around talking with a group of fellow black belts, someone asked, "What does it take to become a great martial arts teacher?"

After the question was asked, the group turned and looked at me. This was probably not only because I was one of the most senior black belts in the group, but I was also one of its biggest philosophers.

After pausing to think for a few moments, I came up with the following answer:

"One becomes great at being a martial arts teacher the same way one becomes great at anything.

"First, know your why. Ask yourself, why do I want to teach martial arts? Knowing your why makes the how a lot easier.

"Second, build your belief in your ability to teach. You cannot succeed at something you don't believe you can succeed at. You can build your beliefs by doing step three."

"The third step is to take action, including getting the best coaching possible. It's much easier to climb Mount Everest if you have a Sherpa to guide you. Find your Sherpa."

"Fourth and finally, practice, practice, practice. Everyone starts at the beginning. Be willing to be less than perfect right now. Then take the feedback you receive on a daily basis to become better and better at whatever you are attempting to accomplish."

Back to the Beginning

So why do you get up in the morning?

What do you want to be remembered for?

As for me, my outcome has changed. Now my purpose is to educate and motivate every person I possibly can how to live in a peak performance state so they can create and live the life of their dreams.

That's what I hope I've done for you.

As we finish our journey together, let me ask you another question.

Do you believe you can do what you want to do?

If you've adopted the strategies in this book, I'm positive you are well on your way to having a rock-solid belief in yourself and your ability to learn everything you need to accomplish your purpose.

Now that you know what you want and believe you can do it, don't wait.

As **Steve Jobs** told us, *"Live every day as if it were going to be your last. Because some day it will be."*

You don't know how much time you have been given on this wonderful planet we call Earth. Take advantage of every precious moment you have.

Stop hesitating. Begin now.

There is no better time than the present moment to start bringing out the peak performer inside of you.

Finally, start practicing. As **Bruce Lee** once said, *"If you spend too much time thinking about a thing, you'll never get it done."*

Now that you've decided what you want, begin and give it all you got.

This is what all peak performers do and is why they are able to accomplish all they do.

Do your very best, and take the feedback you receive to get a little better, every day.

That's all you, or anyone else, can expect of you.

You can use these same four steps to become great at anything. Following them will lead you down the path to peak performance – not just for today, but for the rest of your life.

This is what I want for you.

Thank You!

Thank you for reading my book. I hope you enjoyed it. More than that, I hope you are actually using it to steer yourself in the direction of success, however you define it.

As you do, I want you to remember that becoming the best you is a lifelong process. My wish for you is that you take advantage of every opportunity you have to be the best you possible and, for the rest of your life, live as much as possible in the zone.

If you'd like more information about Mindful Mastery, you can find it on my website http//www.MindfulMindHacking.com.

Like I said, I really hope you got a lot out of this book and I'd like to ask a quick favor.

I would really appreciate it if you could leave me a positive review on Amazon.

I love getting feedback from my customers and reviews on Amazon really do make a difference. I read all my reviews and would really appreciate your thoughts.

Thanks so much.

Wishing you only success!

Wil Dieck

August 20, 2020

Endnotes

1. Kuhn, Thomas (1962). The Structure of Scientific Revolutions (PDF). Chicago: The University of Chicago Press. p. 3. ISBN 9780226458113.

2. Deci, E. L. & Flaste, R. (1996). Why do we do what we do: Understanding Self-Motivation. Penguin Books.

3. R. Ryan and E. Deci, "Self-Determination Theory and the Facilitation of Intrinsic Motivation, Social Development, and Well-being" American Psychologist 55 (2000) 68-78

4. R. Ryan and E. Deci, "Self-Determination Theory and the Facilitation of Intrinsic Motivation, Social Development, and Well-being" American Psychologist 55 (2000) 68-78

5. E.J. Langer and J Rodin (1976). The Effects of Choice and Enhanced Personal Responsibility of the Aged: A Field Experiment in an Institutional Setting. Journal of Personality and Social Psychology 34 (1976): 191-198.

6. Rosenthal R, and Jacobson L., (1968) *Pygmalion in the Classroom: Teacher expectations and pupils' intellectual development.* New York: Holt, Reinhart and Winston

7. Martens, J.P. Tracy, J.L, & Shariff, A.F. (2012). Status signals: adaptive benefits of displaying and observing the nonverbal expressions of pride and shame. Cognitions and Emotions, 26, 390-406

8. Tracy, J.P., Matsumoto, D. (2008). The spontaneous expression of pride and shame: Evidence for biologically innate nonverbal displays. Proceedings of the National Academy of Sciences, 105, 11655-11660.

9. Phillip D. Tomporowski. Effects of acute bouts of exercise on cognition, Acta Psychologica, Volume 112, Issue 3, March 2003, Pages 297–324

10. Raffaella Molteni, Jun-Qi Zheng, Zhe Ying, Fernando Gómez-Pinilla, and Jeffery L. Twiss. Voluntary exercise increases axonal regeneration from sensory neurons, PNAS, Proceedings of the National Academy of Sciences, Published online 2004, May 24

11. Astrid Bjørnebekk, Aleksander A. Mathé, Stefan Brené. International Journal of Neuropsychopharmacology, September 2005, Volume 8, Issue 3, Pp. 357 – 36

Other Books in This Series

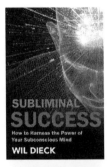

Subliminal Success:
How to Harness the Power of
Your Subconscious Mind

The Secrets of the Black
Belt Mindset: Turning Simple
Habits Into Extraordinary Success

Made in the USA
Middletown, DE
09 September 2020